The Dialogue of Worship

Creating Space for
Revelation and Response

Gary A. Furr
Milburn Price

SMYTH & HELWYS
PUBLISHING, INC.
MACON, GEORGIA

ISBN 1-57312-159-2

The Dialogue of Worship
Creating Space for Revelation and Response

Gary A. Furr and Milburn Price

Copyright © 1998
Smyth & Helwys Publishing, Inc.
6316 Peake Road
Macon, Georgia 31210-3960
1-800-747-3016

Library of Congress Cataloging-in-Publication Data
Furr, Gary.
The dialogue of worship: creating space for revelation and
response. / Gary A. Furr, Milburn Price.
p. cm.—(Faithgrowth: 2)
Includes bibliographical references.
ISBN 1-57312-159-2   (alk. paper)
1. Public worship. I. Price, Milburn. II. Title. III. Series.
BV15.F87 1998
264—dc21   97-50023
                                                                CIP

Contents

95004

Editor's Note

As the general editor of the *FaithGrowth* series, I am pleased to introduce Gary Furr and Milburn Price, the authors of this second volume.

As a Christian educator, I doubt the church *has* a curriculum. Rather, I am committed to the idea that the church *is* a curriculum. Such a distinction represents more than a semantic exercise by a professional educator. The distinction is enormously significant. Worship is a primary illustration of this significance.

Worship has a formative influence in the life of the person of faith. The music of worship creates lifelong connectors for the believer. The affective qualities of worship are not equaled by any other weekly experience. Dramatic potentialities in worship are extraordinary. But rarely do we talk about the curriculum of the worship experience. Who then is qualified to lead that dialogue? I conclude that a pastor and a minister of music who plan and implement worship on a weekly basis are qualified. Ministers who bring the gifts and relationships these two authors bring are supremely qualified.

—William B. Rogers

Preface

Gary Furr and Milburn Price

Collaborating on a book offers multiple possibilities for joint effort. In one model each chapter is produced as the result of shared effort. In another model the work is divided, with each author taking primary responsibility for certain sections, with the other providing review and critique (helpful, of course). This book has emerged from a combination of these two approaches. Most chapters have a primary author. In such cases, the other collaborator has read carefully and responded with both encouragement and suggestion. Chapter 4, however, was a fully collaborative effort—as should be the relationship between pastor and minister of music in worship planning.

The many conversations that led to the shaping of both structure and content for this book—and that guided its development throughout the writing process—took place naturally and happily, as the result of four years' experience of sharing similar conversations focused upon planning the weekly worship services at Vestavia Hills Baptist Church in Birmingham, Alabama. Members of that church helped to influence the book's content through their responses to ideas presented in a series of Wednesday evening sessions in the summer of 1997. To that community of believers we are indebted, not only for this assistance, but also for being a congregation that takes seriously the weekly dialogue of worship and that encourages us continually as we prepare for and lead in that dialogue.

We are grateful to colleagues who read portions of the manuscript at various stages of development and provided insightful reaction and suggestions: They include Dennis Anderson, Minister of Education/Administration at Vestavia Hills Baptist Church; Fisher Humphreys, Professor in the Beeson School of Divinity at Samford University; Paul Richardson, Professor in the School of Music at Samford University; and Stephen Chew, Chair of the Psychology Department at Samford University. Thanks go also to William B. Rogers, editor of this *FaithGrowth* series and Professor at the Baptist Theological Seminary at Richmond, Virginia, for

the invitation to write a book about a subject so much at the heart
of our priorities in ministry and for shepherding the project
toward completion.

To our wives, Vickie and Barbara, we express gratitude for
enduring, with patience, encouragement, and good spirits, the
occasional neglect caused by adding the preparation of a book
manuscript to an already full range of responsibilities and time
demands.

Introduction

Worship as Dialogue and Drama

Milburn Price

In the initial, defining volume of this *FaithGrowth* series, William B. Rogers established "the presence of a dialogic principle coupled with a faithful witness to the Christian story"[1] as one of four foundational guidelines for reflecting on educational ministry in the church. That guideline also serves as a pointer to one of the essential characteristics of Christian worship. For whatever else it may or may not be, worship is a dialogue— one that begins long before a community of believers gathers on a particular day to "worship God," and one that does not end when the sound of the concluding benediction is no longer audible.

This dialogic principle has been suggested in a variety of succinct definitions of worship offered by scholars who have written on the subject over the past six decades:

"Worship . . . is the response of the creature to the Eternal."
—Evelyn Underhill[2]

"Worship is man's [sic] response to God's revelation."
—Andrew W. Blackwood[3]

"Worship is a conversation between the God of revelation and people in need of redemption."
—C. Welton Gaddy[4]

"Liturgy [the 'work of the people' in worship] is an intentionally gathered community in mutual dialogue with God's self-communication."
—Don E. Saliers[5]

"Christian worship is grounded in the reality of the action of God toward the human soul in Jesus Christ and in man's [sic] responsive action through Jesus Christ."
—Paul Waitman Hoon[6]

". . . communion with God."
—Geoffrey Wainwright[7]

Revelation and Response

Ralph Martin has described the "two-beat rhythm of revelation and response" as "the distinctive genius of corporate worship."[8] In applying the definition of worship to its realization in the context of a gathered community of believers, Donald Hustad wrote: "The God-with-people encounters we call 'worship services' should include statements and actions of both *revelation* and *response*."[9] It is these interactive, intertwining elements of *revelation* and *response* that form the substance of most understandings of worship and that will be the focal emphases of this book.

The most frequently cited passage from biblical writings that is illustrative of the revelation-response pattern of worship relates to an individual experience rather than a corporate gathering. Nonetheless, the recounting of Isaiah's "call" recorded in the sixth chapter of Isaiah is instructive in its outline and in its dialogical pattern:

Revelation Isaiah "saw the Lord"—transcendent, "high and lofty," surrounded by seraphim antiphonally extolling God's holiness and glory (vv. 1-4).

Response In light of God's holiness, Isaiah's response was one of contrition, as he recognized his own sinfulness—and that of the surrounding culture—and was moved to confession (v. 5).

Revelation Pardon for sin is symbolized by a seraph touching Isaiah's lips with a live coal taken from the altar. Then the "voice of the Lord" issued a call to service (vv. 6-8a).

Response Isaiah responded in commitment (v. 8b).

Revelation The "voice of the Lord" provided instructions regarding the mission (vv. 9-10).

Response Isaiah asked for clarification of the terms—"How long, O Lord?" (v. 11a). (This questioning aspect of the divine-human encounter is too often overlooked in pious talk about worship and discipleship.)

<u>Revelation</u> The "voice of the Lord" provided greater specificity—with details that must have been discouraging to the prophet (vv. 11b-13).

<u>Response</u> The narrative concerning Isaiah's vision ends here, but the following chapters record Isaiah's fulfillment of his call, with additional occasions of revelation ("the Lord said to me," 8:1) and response ("and I went," 8:3).

Through centuries of evolving worship patterns and traditions, the revelation and response paradigm found in this passage has informed understandings of worship and influenced worship forms—in both liturgical and nonliturgical approaches. Descriptions of the experiences of worshiping communities found in both the Old and New Testaments provide illustrations of its relevance for corporate worship. The application of the structure of Isaiah's experience to the devotional life of communities of believers today provides a model for corporate reenactments of the kind of divine-human encounters essential for maturing spirituality ("faithgrowth").

Dialogue Within the Community

Though the divine-human dialogue is central to an understanding of worship, there is another "conversation" within the context of worship that should be acknowledged and emulated. In writing to the church at Ephesus, Paul gave an admonition to "speak to one another with psalms, hymns and spiritual songs" (Eph 5:19, NIV). The presence of this horizontal direction of communication—from worshipers to worship leaders or from worshiper(s) to worshiper(s)—in the early church is evident from New Testament allusions to the holy kiss (1 Cor 16:20), exhortation and encouragement (Heb 10:24-25), and testimony, of which baptism was a symbolic expression. The continuation of these practices in the mid-second century A.D. is described in passages from Justin Martyr's first Apology: "Our prayers being ended, we greet one another with a kiss."…"Thereafter [following the Eucharist, or Lord's Supper] we continually remind one another of these things."[10]

Worship as Drama

Writers about worship have often cited Søren Kierkegaard's analogy that likens worship to a play. As the analogy is customarily interpreted, congregants are the "actors," worship leaders are the "prompters," and God is present as the "critical theatergoer" (or audience).[11] This analogy is generally used to emphasize the importance of the congregation as participants rather than as spectators. God is present for the occasion, but more as observer than as active participant. Indeed, at one point, Kierkegaard wrote that God "looks on to see how the lines are spoken."[12] If this were all, the entire emphasis would seem to focus upon response. There would be no *revelation*, in which God enters into the drama as full participant, along with the congregants.

In explicating his analogy, however, Kierkegaard suggested that, as a worshiper listens to parts of the "worship script" not requiring active response, in the ideal mode of involvement that worshiper "secretly talks with God."[13] Here the language suggests interactive communication. The emphasis is not upon talking *to* God, but *with* God. There is anticipated dialogical give-and-take. Both revelation and response are present.

Like Kierkegaard, Erik Routley also drew upon images of the theater to interpret the meaning of worship. In his unique, assertive style he wrote: "Worship is drama. It cannot be anything else. It is corporate action."[14] In clarifying his use of this analogy, Routley said, "The essence of drama [as related to worship] is not in the entertainment of a passive audience, but in the involvement of a community in a total response to the fundamental data [God]."[15] Though in this succinct statement he focused upon the *responsive* aspects of the drama of worship, in other parts of *Words*,

Music, and the Church Routley amply explored its *revelatory* dimensions.

With the exception of some improvisatory theater, at the heart of good drama is a good script. If the concept of worship as drama is to be realized in the process of structuring potentially meaningful worship services for a community of believers, the role of the "script" (spoken words, sung words, actions ["stage directions"], non-texted music, planned silence) is crucial. Whether the "script" is carefully crafted in minute detail or partially extemporized, careful attention must be given to its shape and development. It is the "script" that must provide opportunities for both revelation and response. It is the "script" that should give a sense of direction and flow. It is the "script" that ensures appropriate connectedness of the dialogue. And it is the "script" that leads the community at the conclusion of a worship service, not to a final curtain, but to an "until we meet again" intermission.

At this point a caveat is necessary: even the most carefully crafted "script making" cannot guarantee meaningful worship. It is the work of God's Spirit in the midst of the community, facilitating the dialogue, that enables authentic worship. Nonetheless, this truth does not excuse worship planners and leaders from investing the time and effort required to create optimum opportunities for the work of the Spirit. That is the goal of "script making" for worship.

A major part of this book explores issues related to "script making." Chapter 1 treats those aspects of worship that involve the dialogue between the worshiping community and God. Chapter 2 deals with the dialogue that takes place within the worshiping community. Chapter 3 considers the role of music in facilitating the varied strands of conversation that comprise the overall dialogue. Chapter 4 offers suggestions to those who bear the responsibility for worship planning. In Chapter 5 consideration is given to the dialogue of worship as it takes place in settings other than the weekly gatherings of a community of faith. Finally, some summarizing and concluding observations are made.

One final word of introduction: Any observer of worship patterns and practices is aware that styles and forms of worship currently used are both numerous and widely varied. The purpose of this book is to treat substance rather than style, function rather than form. Illustrative allusions are made to practices from divergent worship styles. Worship leaders who find resonance with the dialogical model advocated in these pages may use their own creativity to design ways to implement it within their own traditions.

Notes

[1]William B. Rogers, *Being a Christian Educator: Discovering Your Identity, Heritage, and Vision* (Macon GA: Smyth & Helwys Publishing, Inc., 1996) 28.

[2]Evelyn Underhill, *Worship* (New York: Harper & Brothers [Harper Torchbook Edition], 1957) 3.

[3]Andrew W. Blackwood, *The Fine Art of Public Worship* (Nashville: Abingdon Press, 1939) 14.

[4]C. Welton Gaddy, *The Gift of Worship* (Nashville: Broadman Press, 1992) xvii.

[5]Don E. Saliers, *Worship as Theology: Foretaste of Glory Divine* (Nashville: Abingdon Press, 1994) 26.

[6]Paul Waitman Hoon, *The Integrity of Worship* (Nashville: Abingdon Press, 1971) 77.

[7]Geoffrey Wainwright, *Doxology: The Praise of God in Worship, Doctrine, and Life* (New York: Oxford University Press, 1980) 20.

[8]Ralph Martin, *The Worship of God* (Grand Rapids: Wm. B. Eerdmans Publishing Co., 1982) 6.

[9]Donald Hustad, "The Minister as Worship Leader," *Formation for Christian Ministry*, 3rd ed., ed. Anne Davis and Wade Rowatt, Jr. (Louisville KY: Review and Expositor, 1988) 190.

[10]Justin Martyr, "The First Apology of Justin Martyr," in *Liturgies of the Western Church*, ed. Bard Thompson (Cleveland OH: Meridian Books, 1961) 8-9.

[11]Søren Kierkegaard, *Purity of Heart Is to Will One Thing*, trans. Douglas V. Steere (New York: Harper & Row [Harper Torchbook ed.], 1956) 181.

[12]Ibid.

[13]Ibid.

[14]Erik Routley, *Words, Music, and the Church* (Nashville: Abingdon Press, 1968) 129-30.

[15]Ibid., 177.

Chapter 1

The Community in Dialogue with God

Milburn Price

As a community of Christian believers gathers to worship God, that community participates—both individually and corporately—in a continuing conversation. The conversation began for each believer when he or she first became aware of the prompting of God's Spirit preparing heart and mind to hear and receive the "Word of God." When that hearing and receiving led to an expression of faith in Jesus Christ and a commitment to Jesus as Lord of life, the lifelong pattern of hearing and responding to the "Word of God" was established. It is likely that varying patterns of dialogue with God will be represented within the community. For some believers, intense in their piety and disciplined in its expression, conversation with God is frequent.[1] For others it has become sporadic or intermittent.

For the corporate community the conversation taking place on any given Sunday has a history. That history includes the past experiences of persons related to that particular church. Those experiences—unless the church is a relatively new one—may well antedate the memories of all its members. Indeed, in the broadest sense, a worshiping community at any given point in time is, as it worships, participating in the "communion of saints" extending from the early church to the present by gathering to worship God in the name of Jesus Christ. In large urban congregations, the conversation is likely to be enriched by an aggregate of worshipers whose individual experiences represent a wide variety of places, circumstances, and perhaps even styles.

Hearing the Word of God

Worshipers gather as a community of faith with the expectation not only of responding to God, but also of "hearing a word from the Lord." Within Christian communities there is a sense in which all words have the purpose of illuminating the significance and purposes of "the Word who became flesh"—the incarnate Christ, in whose name the community has gathered. For many who worship in evangelical churches there is a predisposition that they will encounter that "word" primarily from the scripture and sermon. But the possibilities of revelation are varied, for those whose hearts and minds are attuned.

Scripture

In many churches the reading of scripture is concluded by the reader saying, "This is the Word of God for the people of God," to which the congregation responds, "Thanks be to God." These statements reflect the widely held belief of Christians that to each generation the Bible communicates the Word of God in ways that, through the interpretive work of the Holy Spirit, can be understood and followed.

The importance of scripture as a vehicle for revelation is long-standing. In the Jewish synagogue tradition, which strongly influenced the content of early Christian worship, the centrality of the reading of scripture reflected a concern for "the preservation and propagation of the Word of the Lord."[2] Readings from the Law and Prophets, along with prayers, formed the core of synagogue worship.

Descriptions of worship in the New Testament are fragmentary rather than systematized. The fact that early Christians worshiped in the synagogue until the issue of Jesus' identity as Messiah forced them out[3] presumably gave the reading of scripture an influential place in the development of early Christian worship models.[4] Paul's admonition to Timothy regarding "the public reading of Scripture" (1 Tim 4:13) reflects the importance of the practice. It is apparent that Paul expected at least some of his letters to be read to congregations (Col 4:16; 1 Thess 5:27).

The continued pattern of reading scripture in the mid-second century—by that time including some of the texts that have since

become part of the New Testament—is described by Justin
Martyr in his *First Apology*:

> On the day which is called Sunday, all who live in the cities or in
> the countryside gather together in one place. And the memoirs
> of the apostles or the writings of the prophets are read as long as
> there is time.[5]

Given the clear precedent for the reading of scripture in worship, and given the importance attributed to scripture as the
"Word of God," it seems curious that in a number of evangelical
churches the weekly reading of scripture is limited to a few verses
heard immediately before the sermon. By contrast, in other worship traditions one might encounter an Old Testament lesson, a
Gospel lesson, and an Epistle reading in the same service, as well
as the reading or singing of a psalm. For settings in which the
reading of scripture in worship is minimal in current practice, the
inclusion of additional readings would be appropriate. The use of
a lectionary can provide helpful guidance to the inclusion of a
wider scope of scripture readings.

Music

The roles of music in worship are multifaceted. These will be discussed in broader terms in chapter 3, but because it is perhaps its
least recognized function, it is important to address the revelatory
role of music at this point. The stunning account given in the fifth
chapter of 2 Chronicles of the dedication of the temple witnesses
to the potential power of music to lead worshipers into a sense of
God's presence:

> All the levitical singers . . . arrayed in fine linen, with cymbals,
> harps, and lyres, stood east of the altar with one hundred twenty
> priests who were trumpeters. It was the duty of the trumpeters
> and singers to make themselves heard in unison, in praise and
> thanksgiving to the Lord, "For he is good, for his steadfast love
> endures forever," the house, the house of the Lord, was filled

with a cloud, so that the priests could not stand to minister because of the cloud; for the glory of the Lord filled the house of God. (vv. 12-14)

For worshipers sensitive to the aesthetic dimensions of well-crafted music performed convincingly, experiencing such a moment in the context of worship can serve as a vivid reminder of God the Creator, who, in fashioning humankind in the divine image, graced persons with their own creative gifts. As Robert Mitchell noted in *Ministry and Music*, "Through the arts, especially through music, the transcendent, the ineffable, the incomprehensible may be encountered as God's Spirit brings revelation to our human spirit."[6]

In an even more direct way, music can serve as a vehicle for revelation when it persuasively conveys biblical texts communicating the "Word of God" and when it presents extrabiblical texts in ways that illuminate faith. Theologian Oscar Cullman demonstrated a sensitivity to this dialogical role of music in writing:

> Johann Sebastian Bach has made it possible for us to hear, in the the Credo of the *Mass in B Minor*, the musical interpretation of the words of this ancient creed which faithfully reproduces the New Testament faith in Christ's resurrection and our own. . . . And Handel, in the last part of the *Messiah*, gives us some inkling of what Paul understood by the sleep of those who rest in Christ.[7]

Anthems, vocal solos, and vocal ensemble selections can all provide persuasive communication when texts that have been given appropriate musical settings are performed in a manner that reflects preparation in rehearsal and concern for the effective delivery of those texts.

Sermon*

Preaching is the proclamation of the good news of Jesus Christ through the words of ordinary messengers. From the earliest days of the Christian church until the present, despite recurring criticisms that it is irrelevant and outdated, preaching continues to hold a significant role in Christian worship.

The first aims of preaching are to proclaim Jesus Christ and to elicit a response from the hearer. As Erik Routley noted, it is not necessarily the preacher's task to determine the exact nature of that response, but the point of preaching *is* to lead to some type of response.[8]

In the New Testament, preaching is central both in the ministry of Jesus and in the early church. New Testament scholar C. H. Dodd has claimed persuasively that the heart of the Christian message is conveyed through preaching. The New Testament writers, he said, make a distinction between preaching and teaching. The latter concerns ethical and doctrinal instruction, whereas preaching is the public proclamation of Christianity to a non-Christian world. This message, said Dodd, focused on the cross and resurrection of Christ. If we study the sermons in the book of Acts, for example, we see there the very core of the Christian message of salvation.[9]

The New Testament scripture itself was shaped by having been preached before it was written down. The Gospels and the Letters were written, not in long, seamless narratives, but in short units that are perfectly suited for preaching.

Preaching has changed and adapted through the ages, surviving diverse styles, adaptations, and experiments, but its essential purpose has not changed. Every preacher of the Christian faith stands in the pulpit convinced that "in Christ God was reconciling the world to himself (2 Cor 5:19).

The "scripting" of preaching can, like a bad play, be predictable and dull. Even worse, it can be manipulative. A play is said to be "preachy" when it uses the medium of drama to coerce a certain (and unvarying) response. Good preaching is direct, understandable, and dynamic, but it also has a certain quality of open-endedness. It is evocative—it stirs and "opens up" without substituting for the work of the Spirit.

Preaching is, in this day, a form of corporate spiritual guidance. Preachers must be spiritual guides for their congregations. At the least, preachers must attend to their own spiritual lives in order to help others. These times require—as perhaps all times do—that preachers know something about guidance and direction.[10]

Believers understand that the sermon is a vehicle through which God speaks in worship in a distinctive way. Preaching, too, is a conversation—a series of deep dialogues in which the miracle of divine communication to human beings continues to take flesh. In the act of preaching, the eternal Word of God connects to the present moment of worship through the proclaimer's words and life.

In this way, we see that in preaching the conversations of a group of believers intersect. Good preaching grows out of attentive listening to the Word of God in study as well as listening to the congregation's situation and needs.

Silence

It does not seem coincidental that Jaroslav Vajda's evocative hymn text, "Now the Silence,"[11] which imaginatively enumerates many of the images and actions of worship, begins with silence. Silence has long occupied an important role in both individual and corporate worship. Its presence implies the fulfillment of a biblical admonition: "The Lord is in his holy temple; let all the earth keep silence before him" (Hab 2:20). In some current worship practices, however, silence has become all but lost. Many churches whose worship is strongly influenced by revivalist traditions have dispensed with silence as "too liturgical." Other contemporary churches from a wide variety of denominational traditions, whose weekly worship practices have been shaped by either the demands of radio and television production or the influence of the television medium, have abandoned silence as a component of corporate worship from the mistaken assumption that it creates "dead time"—either in the broadcast/telecast of the service or in the flow of worship elements.

To the contrary, appropriate moments of silence contribute to the rhythm of revelation and response in worship by providing "waiting space" for the revelatory work of God's Spirit. Writing in

Walking on Water, Madeleine L'Engle said: "Deepest communion with God is beyond words, on the other side of silence."[12] A church that takes seriously the concept of worship as dialogue must also take seriously the role of silence within the context of worship. Given the variety of individual needs and circumstances brought to the worship gathering, it is impossible for worship planners to craft a "worship script" that brings the uniquely appropriate "Word of the Lord" for that day to each individual. Certainly, the major emphases of corporate worship can be reiterated weekly—and these can have both value and relevance to the worshiping community in their repetition.

But what of the longings of the heart of individual worshipers that may not be touched by these themes on a given day? Where can they be met? *Within the silence!* It is in the silence that God's Spirit can speak the "gentle whisper" (1 Kgs 19:12b, NIV) that inaudibly touches the heart and mind—individually. It is in the silence that individual worshipers can strain to hear the "Word of the Lord" that speaks to their particular needs—without the distractions of words or music. Welton Gaddy summarized the matter well:

> In worship, silence is far more than an absence of sound. Silence constitutes a vital part of the divine-human dialogue. In silence, worshipers can experience interchanges with God that will not be known where silence does not prevail.[13]

Symbols

The presence of symbols in a place of worship acknowledges that the eye can be an important instrument to receive God's revelation. Scenes depicting Old Testament stories, as well as the early church at worship, were found on the walls of Roman catacombs. In medieval cathedrals, stained-glass pictures served to remind congregants of biblical stories when illiteracy prevented them from reading and rereading the stories for themselves.

The symbol of the fish was used by the early church to provide a reminder to believers of Jesus' call to discipleship. *Ixthus*,

the Greek word for fish, created an acrostic that summarized the
essential core of faith:[14]

I	[*Iesous*]	Jesus
X	[*Christos*]	Christ
θ	[*Theos*]	God's
Y	[*Uios*]	Son
Σ	[*Soteros*]	Savior

Though the primary use of this symbol among early Christians
seems to have been outside the context of worship, it nonetheless
exemplifies the power of symbols to communicate Christian truth
in a nonverbal form.

Visual art flourished in both Eastern and Western branches of
the Christian church during the medieval era. Magnificently
crafted cathedrals, pictures created in stained glass, ornately
carved furnishings (pulpit, altar), and artistically designed chalices
all sought to symbolize the grandeur and majesty of the God
being worshiped.

In spite of the restrictions imposed on the use of art and symbol in worship spaces by the Calvinist and Zwinglian influences of
the Reformation movement, there remains at least a modest
display of symbols today in most evangelical churches. The communion table, the architectural display of a cross, biblical or
historical persons or scenes depicted in stained-glass windows, and
the open Bible all communicate symbolically. A number of
churches in recent years have drawn upon the revelatory possibility of symbols by creating banners for placement in the worship
center during the changing seasons of the Christian year. Of the
communicative role of symbols, William B. Rogers wrote: "They
teach both the inquisitive mind and the wandering mind."[15]

Drama

In recent years many churches have rediscovered the potential of
drama as a vehicle for presenting the Word of God. The use of
brief dramatic vignettes to enact biblical stories was introduced

into Christian worship as early as the tenth century. The earliest of these dramas, complete with costumes, properties, and limited "stage action," dealt with events surrounding the resurrection of Jesus, and that event remained the most popular subject for musico-dramatic presentations through the thirteenth century. During this time, however, a variety of other subjects were also given dramatic depiction.[16]

Dramatic scenes, utilized carefully and thoughtfully within the overall "drama of worship," can still be used to present God's Word, whether enacting biblical stories, as in the medieval church dramas, or portraying dramatic situations related to contemporary living. The same cautions should be applied as were suggested for music, however. Drama, whenever used, should relate to the dialogic pattern of worship and should not be an intrusion or diversion for the sake of entertainment.

Responding to the Word of God

Upon encountering God's revelation, believers should feel themselves moved to respond. Within the context of corporate worship that response may occur through several modes.

Praise

"The beginning and end of all worship is the praise of God." This truism rightly focuses upon praise as an essential ingredient in responses to God. Indeed, praise is imbedded in the meaning of *weorthscipe*, the Anglo-Saxon predecessor from which the English word "worship" was derived. Its meaning is "to ascribe worth," as in the declarations of the apocalyptic hymns found in Revelation:

> You are worthy, our Lord and God, to receive glory and honor and power, for you created all things, and by your will they existed and were created. (4:11)

Worthy is the Lamb that was slaughtered to receive power and wealth and wisdom and might and honor and glory and blessing! (5:12)

The psalmist wrote, "Ascribe to the Lord the glory due his name" (Ps 96:8). The Hebrew word translated as "glory" can be interpreted as "honor"; thus, the writer of the psalm included the ascription of honor to God among the attributes of worship. At the birth of Jesus, angels sang "Glory to God in the highest" (Luke 2:14).

Praise in Christian worship is multifaceted. Its scope embraces a variety of attitudes: acknowledgement of God's holiness and majesty, adoration, awe, blessing, and gratitude. Its mood ranges from quiet reflection to exuberant celebration. It may be expressed, in differing worship traditions, through spoken word, song, instrumental music, exclamation (the "hallelujahs" of Revelation 19 are illustrative), and gesture (Ps 134:2).

Praise in Christian worship, at its fullest and most complete, is Trinitarian in direction, as it acknowledges the creative, redemptive, and empowering work of God. Though all of these themes may not appear in each worship service, it is essential that each finds expression recurringly.[17] In differing worship traditions Trinitarian affirmations are found in the singing of the "Doxology" and "Gloria Patri" (each with its ascription of praise to "Father, Son, and Holy Ghost"), in baptismal rites, in hymns and choruses, in the Apostles' and Nicene Creeds, and in the reading of numerous New Testament passages.

Confession of Sin

When Isaiah "saw the Lord" (Isa 6:1) and became aware of his own condition in contrast to God's majesty and holiness, he was moved to confess both his own sin and the sin of the surrounding culture. Since early in the development of Christian worship forms, a confessional element has been present. In liturgical churches it was expressed in *Kyrie eleison, Christe eleison, Kyrie eleison* ("Lord, have mercy; Christ, have mercy; Lord, have mercy") and in *Agnus Dei, qui tollis peccata mundi, miserere nobis* ("Lamb of God, who takes away the sins of the world, have mercy on us").

Perhaps the placement of the *Kyrie* early in the liturgical format sprang from the continuing influence of the *Didache*, an instructional manual dating from the late first century or early second century, which prescribed: "On the Lord's Day, come together, break bread, and give thanks, having first confessed your transgressions, that your sacrifices may be pure."[18]

Biblical foundations for the need for confession of sin are abundant (for example, Lev 5:5; 26:40; Num 5:6-7; Ps 32:5; 1 John 1:9). In spite of these varied admonitions, confession of sin has not found a place in the corporate worship of many evangelical churches. Perhaps this absence is the result of an overreaction to the prominence given to confession in liturgical worship. Perhaps it is because of an assumption that the primary role of confession of sin is related to that initial confession that leads to acceptance of Jesus Christ as Lord and Savior. If the latter alternative is the case, it may be instructive to note that the admonition found in 1 John 1:9 ("If we confess our sins, he who is faithful and just will forgive us our sins and cleanse us from all unrighteousness") was written to believers.

Within the context of the worshiping community, confession of sin can be expressed in a variety of ways. It can be *sung*, using appropriate texts set to music for congregational song. John Greenleaf Whittier's "Dear Lord and Father of Mankind," "No, Not Despairingly" by Horatius Bonar, and the familiar gospel hymn "Whiter than Snow" are illustrative of hymns that would fulfill this function.

Confession of sin can be expressed through *congregational readings*. Either unison readings or responsive readings—particularly litanies—can serve to allow the worshiping community to voice confession together.

Perhaps the most effective medium for confession of sin in corporate worship is *silence*—in response to scripture, a spoken call to confession, a musical call to confession, or a sermon. Silence allows the expression of confession to God to be individualized. It helps to remove, or at least minimize, an excessive sense of self-consciousness.

Thanksgiving

Thanksgiving is a natural outgrowth of the act of remembering (*anamnesis*), which is an essential component of biblically-based worship. In responding to a recollection of God's creative power and salvific acts, it has been the pattern of both Old Testament and New Testament worship that God's people give thanks. Central to Old Testament temple worship was the offering of sacrifices of praise and thanksgiving. The concluding section of the *tefillah*—a series of prayers from the synagogue worship tradition—offered thanks to God. Allusions to the expression of thanksgiving in Paul's letters (1 Cor 10:30; 14:16; 1 Tim 4:4) suggest its practice in the early church. Embedded in liturgies of the Eucharist (which, in itself, means "thanksgiving") from their embryonic forms were prayers of thanksgiving.[19]

Don Saliers suggests that the offering of thanksgiving may even facilitate the experience of new revelation: "When authentic praise and thanksgiving are offered in response to the divine initiative, the conditions for receiving the divine self-communication are made alive."[20] Whatever its ancillary effects may be, the recurring expression of gratitude forms an essential component of believers' responses to God.

Offering

The practice of bringing offerings (of monetary resources) to worship is prompted by an understanding that believers are called to be faithful stewards of all of God's gifts. The act of "bringing an offering" of monetary value, in that context, becomes both a tangible response to God's graciousness and a symbol of the broader commitment of the totality of life.[21] Indeed, worship as a whole may be viewed in this manner.

In the early church the inherited Old Testament traditions of sacrificial offerings were reinterpreted in light of Jesus' sacrifice of life.[22] Offerings both in New Testament references (Matt 6:1-4 and Acts 24:17, for example) and in the early church were used primarily to minister to human needs. In Justin Martyr's *First Apology* appears the following account:

> Those who are prosperous, if they wish, contribute what each one deems appropriate; and the collection is deposited with the president; and he takes care of the orphans and widows, and those who are needy . . .[23]

Jesus' own self-emptying provides a model for the broader understanding of "offering," or stewardship. That model is suggested in Paul's appeal to the Romans "to present your bodies as a living sacrifice, holy and acceptable to God—which *is your spiritual worship*" (Rom 12:1). Such an understanding allows the concept of offering to embrace time and abilities, as well as material resources.

Petition and Intercession

Through prayers of petition (requests for divine assistance in matters of personal concern) and intercession (prayers on behalf of the broader needs of the world) worshipers participate in God's continuing work in the world. Such prayers spring from a confidence that the God who has acted in the past continues to act in the present. They also suggest a response to Jesus' invitation to "ask, and it will be given you" (Matt 7:7).

Both petition and intercession were present in the prayers of the synagogue tradition, which strongly influenced the worship of the early church. The seventeenth chapter of John's Gospel provides a poignant example of Jesus praying on behalf of others. "Prayers of the faithful" (intercessory prayers) have long held a central place in eucharistic rites. Saliers cogently observed, "Prayers for others in the context of Christian liturgy show a fundamental christological orientation: as Christ had compassion, so must we."[24]

Concerning prayers of petition and intercession, Ralph Martin wrote: "Prayer 'succeeds' when it melts into commitment and obedience; it fails when it is treated as a recital of our needs and an attempt to force God to act."[25] The desired result of such prayers should be the mobilization of worshipers for acts of service that address some of the needs enumerated.

Commitment

An encounter with the "Word of God" may lead to a renewal of commitment—or a response to that Word as it has been encountered on that particular occasion. It is a common practice of evangelical churches to move toward the conclusion of the worship service, following the sermon, by singing a "hymn of invitation." The text of the hymn is typically one that conveys initial acceptance of Jesus as Savior and Lord ("Just As I Am" and "I Hear Thy Welcome Voice," for example). Though hymns of this type are certainly appropriate for evangelistic services, for the weekly worship services of a community of faith the full flow of worship is better served by the choice of a hymn that enables worshipers to voice a response to the "Word of God" as it has been proclaimed in that service.

Opportunities for worshipers to express renewed commitments—or new commitments based upon fresh insights into the claims of discipleship—within the context of worship contribute to the continuing process of spiritual formation. Marva Dawn addressed this aspect of worship in writing, "Worship is meant to usher us into God's presence so that we can delight in that relationship *and consequently be formed to live according to God's best purposes.*"[26]

Table Talk

There was a time in American culture—a more relaxed time—when in many homes the family meal was an important occasion. News was shared. Relationships were nurtured. Dialogue and dining were intermingled. When a Christian community gathers at the Table of the Lord, sharing in the Eucharist ("thanksgiving"), or Lord's Supper, these same characteristics should be present.

The key to their being so is the dialogue—along with the disposition of the hearts of the worshipers.

At the Table, the Word of the Lord is received through both scripture and symbol. It is customary for the observance of the Lord's Supper to include the reading of the Words of Institution from one of the Gospels (Matt 26:26-29; Mark 14:22-25; or Luke 22:19-20) or from Paul's first letter to the Corinthian church (1 Cor 11:23-26). In settings in which the Words of Institution are not read, at least some of the words of Jesus are usually repeated by the worship leader immediately prior to the worshipers' partaking of the elements: "Take and eat; this is my body" and "This is my blood of the covenant, which is poured out for many for the forgiveness of sins."

Meanwhile, throughout the observance, the bread and cup stand as symbols—visual reminders of the overflowing love and magnificent grace that were expressed in the crucifixion and death of Jesus. Somewhere in the worship center there also may be a cross that serves as another symbol of that event.

In these ways the Word of God comes to the worshiping Christian community during the Eucharist. Through word and symbol news has been shared. We call it the gospel ("good news").

And what of the worshipers' part of the dialogue at the Table? It may be expressed in words (a litany of response provided by the "script writers" for the service), song (using an appropriate hymn or chorus of response), actions (receiving and partaking of the elements), and the silent murmerings of the heart. Authentic participation in the dialogue and involvement in the drama symbolized at the Table nurture the relationship between the believer and God.

Notes

[1]More will be said about the forms and methods of personal dialogue with God in chapter 5.

[2]Robert E. Webber, *Worship Old and New*, rev. ed. (Grand Rapids: Zondervan Publishing House, 1994) 36.

[3]Ibid., 41.

[4]For a discussion of the reading of scripture in early Christian worship, see Ralph P. Martin, *Worship in the Early Church* (Grand Rapids: Wm. B. Eerdmans Publishing Co., 1974) 68-73.

[5]Justin Martyr, "The First Apology of Justin Martyr," in *Liturgies of the Western Church*, ed. Bard Thompson (Cleveland OH: Meridian Books, 1961) 9.

[6]Robert Mitchell, *Ministry and Music* (Philadelphia: Westminster Press, 1978) 91.

[7]Oscar Cullmann, "Immortality of the Soul or Resurrection of the Dead?" in *Immortality and Resurrection*, ed. Krister Stendahl (New York: Macmillan Co., 1965) 53.

[8]Erik Routley, *The Divine Formula* (Princeton: Prestige Publications, 1986) 19.

[9]C. H. Dodd, *The Apostolic Preaching and Its Development* (New York: Harper & Brothers, 1936).

[10]Spiritual direction is a separate endeavor from preaching, but this separation is not absolute. In the Baptist tradition, for example, preaching has been seen to be a primary form of "spiritual direction." See Margaret Guenther, *Holy Listening: The Art of Spiritual Direction* (Boston: Cowley Publications, 1992); Glenn Hinson, "Baptist and Quaker Spirituality," in *Christian Spirituality III: Post-Reformation and Modern*, Louis Dupre, John Meyendorf, and Don Saliers, eds. (New York: Crossroad/Continuum, 1989) 324-38.

[11]Jaroslav J. Vajda, "Now the Silence," in *Now the Joyful Celebration* (St. Louis: Morning Star Music Publishers, 1987) 39. (See p. 47 of the present volume for the complete text.)

[12]Madeleine L'Engle, *Walking on Water: Reflections on Faith and Art* (Wheaton IL: H. Shaw, 1980) 128.

[13]C. Welton Gaddy, *The Gift of Worship* (Nashville: Broadman Press, 1992) 110.

[14]Rey O'Day and Edward A. Powers, *Theatre of the Spirit* (New York: The Pilgrim Press, 1980) 52-53.

[15]William B. Rogers, *Being a Christian Educator* (Macon GA: Smyth & Helwys Publishing, 1996) 71.

[16]For detailed information on this subject, see Karl Young, *The Drama of the Medieval Church*, vol. 1 (Oxford: Clarendon Press, 1933) and William L. Smoldon, "Liturgical Drama," in *Early Medieval Music up to 1300*, vol. 2 of *New Oxford History of Music* (London: Oxford University Press, 1955).

[17]Paul Waitman Hoon has noted: "As a service of Christian worship is authentic only when all its elements are reconcilable with the Trinity,

so thought about worship possesses integrity only when all its elements can be related within the Trinity." *The Integrity of Worship* (Nashville: Abingdon Press, 1971) 115.

[18]Quoted in Geoffrey Wainwright, *Doxology: The Praise of God in Worship, Doctrine, and Life* (New York: Oxford University Press, 1980) 131.

[19]See, for example, the liturgy from Hippolytus (c. 200 A.D.) in Bard Thompson, ed., *Liturgies of the Western Church*, 20-23.

[20]Don E. Saliers, *Worship as Theology* (Nashville: Abingdon Press, 1994) 86.

[21]For more on this matter, see Hoon, 352.

[22]For an extended treatment of offering from both Old Testament and New Testament perspectives, see Martin, *The Worship of God* (Grand Rapids: Wm. B. Eerdmans Publishing Co., 1982) 60-79.

[23]Justin Martyr, 9.

[24]Saliers, 132.

[25]Martin, *The Worship of God*, 37.

[26]Marva J. Dawn, *Reaching Out Without Dumbing Down* (Grand Rapids: Wm. B. Eerdmans Publishing Co., 1995) 116.

*The section "Sermon" was written by Gary Furr.

Chapter 2

The Dialogue
Within the Community

Gary Furr

Worship is, first and foremost, that event in which human beings respond to God. A worship service is also a human experience, however, in which human beings interact with one another.

Some Christians become defensive when the human dimension of their worship is pointed out. In part, they do not wish to concede that their worship is open to examination or question. This sentiment may also express a bias that worship is wholly a "spiritual" event. This concept denies the obvious human element in worship that accounts for both diversity of expression and its many divergent cultural idioms.

The Scriptures, however, do not share this concept. In Revelation 21:3, John's vision of the final glory of heaven is a scene of unending worship around the throne of God. Yet that vision begins with a remarkable declaration: "See, the home of God is among mortals. He will dwell with them as their God; they will be his peoples, and God himself will be with them."

The glory of God is the goal of all life, but God's desire is to be in fellowship with the creation. Therefore, to talk about the dialogue *within* the community is not to suggest something that detracts from or is peripheral to worship. The communion we seek inevitably embodies and touches the relationships of human participants with one another as well as their relationship to God. It communicates shared insights and also depicts cultural commonalities.

This "taking flesh" is at the heart of Christian faith. A worshiping community may either acknowledge this essential humanity in worship honestly or fall prey to unconscious and unreflective worship that is a result of the failure to accept the responsibility that comes with acknowledgement.

The "Curriculum" of Worship

The dialogue within the community is at the heart of ministry. Ministry is service to God through the spiritual nurture of others. Here we find ourselves at the formational end of the term "spiritual formation." "Spiritual" is primarily about relationship with God, but "formation" includes the space and time channels through which that connection is made flesh.

We might, therefore, subtitle this chapter "How Worship Forms People." As mentioned in the first chapter, it is always risky to talk about worship as a means to anything except a response to God. When worship is subverted for pragmatic ends, however noble-sounding, it is no longer worship. When worship is considered as spiritual formation, it is important to remember that this is an ancillary dimension that flows out of the larger purpose of praising and responding to God.

However, it is equally important to acknowledge that in the "scripting" of worship we are also communicating with other human beings. We are saying something about our faith to one another. We inevitably reflect our context, interacting with both our particular place and time. World events and local tragedies may not change the essence of our worship, but the nuances, selections, and emphases of a particular service will exhibit the context of that particular community of faith.

On a practical level, every congregation expresses these relationships in many ways, but often it does so unreflectively. Christian educator Maria Harris observes that every church has a "curriculum"—that is, an accepted "subject matter." Once curriculum was thought to be a very simple matter, confined to the Sunday School and generally considered an "educational" matter.[1]

Now, however, we know that a "curriculum" is broader than that and includes all of the aspects of a church's life. Therefore, when we worship, we are also communicating the "curriculum" of the church. Harris identifies five broad areas of Christian ministry within the church. They are not themselves the curriculum of any particular church, but they are what she calls "curricular forms."

These five—*kerygma* (proclamation), *didache* (teaching), *leitourgia* (worship and prayer), *koinonia* (community), and *diakonia* (service)—are rooted in the Bible and church history and are proven to be essential and core dimensions for Christian ministry.[2] When we come to worship, it helps to ask, "What does our worship express about these five areas?" In the following sections, these five curricula and the ways in which they are enacted in worship are described and analyzed.

Suzanne Johnson points out that a curriculum in a local church can operate on multiple levels—not all of them conscious to the congregation. A church is an entity whose organization, relationships, and interactions are quite complex. Therefore, there may be more than one "curriculum" operative in a single congregation. She suggests that there are three types of curricula that coexist within any congregation.[3]

(1) Every church has an *explicit* curriculum in its worship as well as its educational area. This curriculum operates in a somewhat official nature and is represented by denominational materials, creeds, and/or confessions. The explicit curriculum is observable in the hymns (the "canon" used in that particular church), sermons, accepted and articulated beliefs, and adopted statements and programs in that congregation.

(2) A church also operates with an *implicit* curriculum, consisting of the unspoken and unconscious "rules by which we socialize persons into the congregation."[4] This process impresses upon people what is acceptable or unacceptable to believe, do, feel, or think. In worship it may include the acceptability of musical styles, styles of preaching or testimony, and norms for demonstrative behavior, as well as theological issues that are "acceptable" to talk about and those that are not.

(3) Finally, Johnson says there is the *"null"* curriculum. In a sense this curriculum is a paradox, because it does not actually exist.[5] What is meant by "null curriculum" is that we exclude some aspects of reality, often unconsciously. This exclusion can lead to "compartmentalization" in the church, whereby members live in multiple realities that rarely connect with one another. In some churches members may experience the absence of talk about the

Bible or prayer. In other churches, the "null curriculum" may have to do with issues of sexuality, women's issues, or race. The null curriculum is expressed in worship through the choices of Bible translations, the selection of worship leaders, who is never called on to speak or pray or lead, and sermon themes and texts that are never considered.

Theological candor can be a beginning. As Erik Routley puts it, worship is in part a "handing over" of tradition. We can either betray that tradition or connect it faithfully to the present. A reflective and intentional internal conversation about worship enables worship leaders to understand more adequately the implications of their decisions about script and participants.[6] When we avoid making these decisions public and open to debate, we are likely to fall victim to manipulation, unconscious distortions, and pragmatism in worship.

Kerygma (Proclamation)

Kerygma is usually associated with the proclamation of the gospel through preaching. Proclaiming the gospel is also a conversation of the believing community. This proclamation is enacted more broadly than simply understanding the preacher as a representative figure of the whole community.

In worship, the gospel is proclaimed. It is also remembered and passed on. Part of the task of a community of faith is to hand the stories in the Bible on to others. In this regard, the reading of scripture publicly is essential (and too often disregarded!). Too many evangelical churches confine the reading of scripture to a few verses for the sermon. Faith in the gospel invites the congregation to trust that reading the scriptures (including lengthy passages) in public worship is also an opportunity for a congregation whose contact with the primary stories is decreasing to hear them. Occasionally, this should also involve corporate reading of scripture.

Confession of Faith

Confession of faith is often thought of in individual terms. When we read a confession or creed aloud corporately, however, it is also a defining act of a community in conversation with itself. We are confessing the faith to one another.

These conversations are absolutely essential, for it is by confessing our faith in one form or another that a community clarifies its essential corporate identify. It sets the boundaries of its beliefs, expresses its convictions, and articulates its experience with God.

We see this conversation at work in the early centuries of Christianity in the formation of scripture itself. Christians believe, of course, that the Bible is the Word of God and that it was inspired by God. This collection came into focus, however, over a period of three hundred years as the church used, practiced, debated, and disagreed about which books were scripture.

Definition of the canon was finally essential for a number of reasons. First, as the apostles died, the first generation was lost to the church, and the faith had to be preserved and passed on to the next generation. The theological and practical crisis of the delay of Christ's coming made it essential to preserve the stories and teachings of Jesus.

Second, crises brought on by persecution and rejection by the larger culture made it essential that the scrolls be preserved. Which ones were most essential? The community engaged in conversation.

Third, as several attempts were made to influence the canon in different ways, the church had to resist certain temptations. Against Tatian and his harmony of the Gospels, called the *Diatessaron*, the church resisted the attempt to synthesize the Bible to eliminate difficulties in it artificially. Against the Montanists, a kind of charismatic movement that emphasized individual and subjective revelation, the church affirmed that there were limits to what could be held to be revelation. Against the Gnostics and Marcion, who wanted to shorten the collection to a single Gospel and the letters of Paul and reject the Old Testament, the church affirmed the broader collection.

How did this take place? Scholars still do not know for certain. There are no records of official decisions about it. More likely, the shape of the canon took place as the church used, read, applied, and tested scripture in their lives.[7]

This entire process of canonization is an example of the work of self-defining that the church had to undertake in its internal conversations about who it was, who Jesus was, and what it believed. This kind of process continues now. Churches must always, and not only in preaching, be about the task of defining themselves in the faith.

This self-definition is done partly through confessions and creeds. In responsive readings, litanies, confessions, and creeds, the church "reminds" itself who it is. It is "remembering." Human identity is essentially based on memory. When persons are unable to remember because of aging or disease, their sense of identity begins to slip away.

The same is true of a community of faith. By remembering, we strengthen the sense of identity with the past. More importantly, we also connect that heritage with the present moment. It is "owned" by the individuals present as well. Corporately, confession of faith is "internal conversation" in the community, in which we remind ourselves.

Obviously, the hymns and songs of the church form another primary way that confession of faith takes place. It also takes forms such as personal testimony. Congregations need to hear not only the formal faith of a sermon and the corporate conversation of the confession, but also the personal and often diverse ways in which that identity lives out in particular persons.

Baptism

We can observe this identity process clearly in the act of baptism. In the act of baptism an individual is incorporated into the community. To "incorporate" means, quite literally, to "become part of a body." Incorporation happens primarily through Christian baptism, but this is also a corporate act—the community attests the profession of faith, affirms the person, and welcomes him or her on God's behalf into the community. The theology of baptism and its meaning is far too complex to treat here,[8] but one aspect of baptism, a central one, does need to be mentioned. Baptism is the entry of the individual into the body of the church. In the free church tradition this is done experientially—baptism follows profession. In other traditions it is sometimes done retrospectively, but baptism clearly carries the idea of a rite of passage into a new existence.

In a sense, baptism is a solitary act—one person expresses his or her confession of faith in Jesus Christ. The community has a role to play, however. It hears the confession of faith by the candidate, offers its support, discerns the validity of the conversation, and promises to nurture the person being baptized. In the conversionist churches, of which Baptists are part, baptism is a confession of faith. In the act of baptism candidates "identify" with Christ. They confess their personal faith. It is witnessed and affirmed by the community, which welcomes them into fellowship: "You are now one of us."

Didache (Teaching)

Worship communicates many messages. Some of them are even intended! Whatever our intent, however, every congregation in its worship conveys certain convictions (or the lack of any clear ones). Didache is "teaching." This has usually been understood to be the moral standards and way of life of the Christian community.[9] In worship, the community is concerned with the moral and spiritual formation of its members. Whether the society of which the church is a part upholds these ideals or not, the church gives them voice and teaches them.

Worship is not concerned with content alone, but also involves modeling. Children see how we express our faith and imitate that. Most parents who are active in church have observed small children "playing church." What messages do we send about worship?

Often we are teaching by how we welcome, who comes, what we do (or what everyone understands is forbidden here), and what we never talk about. The dignity, respect, and courtesy toward the worship space, fellow members, and God have a powerful effect upon all who participate.

Not long ago in our congregation a member who has a disability visited another church and brought back a worship guide from the service. He was impressed by the wording about standing for certain portions of the service. Next to the asterisk below, the guide said, "All who are able may stand." It was a simple sentence, but it sent a message: "You are not guilty of non-participation."

One church decided to provide an electric lift for persons using wheelchairs to get to its turn-of-the-century (and nearly inaccessible for ambulatory-impaired persons) sanctuary. Individuals could operate it themselves. Immediately, new participants showed up for worship. A very simple and potent message of recognition had been spoken silently by that action. It told them, "You are not excluded."

We communicate subtle things in our worship in the non-verbal messages. We say things unwittingly about family and children. For example, the trend toward "children's church" in the United States has sent some unintentional messages. First, we are saying, "Children need to be entertained and amused." Second, we are saying, "This is for adults." The irony is that one day children are sent back into the worship service and the fun is over forever! Then they must begin what was formerly ignored—learning how to worship.

Recognition of children in their spiritual passages is a way of naming our perception of God in their lives. This need not be narcissistic—it can be incorporated into worship in significant ways other than "children's sermons," which are often mostly for adults' shortened theological attention spans anyway. We teach something when children are instructed about hymnals and rituals, traditions and practices. Do we, in our various well-intentioned ways, say to children, as the disciples did, "Go away, the Master and his adult disciples are too busy right now"?

In addition to these considerations, of course, are the more explicit ways we teach during the worship time. For example, most congregations read scripture as a part of worship as a way to confess the faith. At issue for the church is the question of "Who reads scripture?" Only men? Only clergy? Only polished and well-trained persons?

Similarly, we face curriculum issues in the issue of selection—how do we decide which scriptures will be read? If a church follows a lectionary, then it is forced to range across the scriptures, even, occasionally, into texts that are less comfortable. If the scriptures are simply selected to agree with the pastor's sermon for the day, it may accomplish thematic consistency, but at the price of breadth and depth. It means that the "canon" of scripture for this congregation is determined by the pastor's particular preferences and themes.

Leitourgia (Worship)

From the angle of the dialogue within the community, the idea of "sacred space" is important. The word "sanctuary" implies safety, shelter, and protection. A worship space communicates an otherness, but also a haven where individuals can come into acceptance, reflection, and space. A congregation is in "inaudible dialogue" simply by the space it provides and the visual, auditory (or silent!), olfactory, tactile, and even taste sensations (for example, the Lord's Supper) worshipers experience.

Communion literally means "in common." Symbolized in those traditions where the Lord's Supper is shared in the common cup, our *koinonia* means a fellowship that is deeper than mere socializing among people who are similar. The common faith, the common kingdom, our common love of the Savior, and our common hope bring us together.

Part of this commonness, however, is in the sharing of our burdens. "Bear one another's burdens, and in this way you will fulfill the law of Christ" (Gal 6:2), wrote Paul. Wise worship leaders always plan with an ear to the sufferings and struggles of the people. Sometimes there are national or international events of such magnitude that all are affected. Worship can give voice and lend comfort to the anxieties and fears of people through responsive readings, pastoral prayers, or even in the simple repetition of liturgy.

Corporate Prayer

Corporate prayer has nearly become a lost art. Curiously, with the modern obsession with informality, intimacy, and personal, experiential religion, corporate prayers have come to be viewed with suspicion, since a meaningful corporate prayer is often composed prior to its being prayed. First, the fact that something is composed "spontaneously," by which we often mean "extemporaneously," does not make it better or more efficacious. As Fred Craddock put it, the Holy Spirit is able to act in the pastor's study as freely as in a public moment.[10] When public prayer is not given thought, it often digresses into unofficial "pet prayers" or oft-repeated "cliché prayers."

Prayer, whether an individual or a corporate prayer litany, is always composed with the congregation in mind. What is it that this community of faith struggles to understand or live? Good prayer grows out of communal listening. Finally, a corporate prayer has more of the form of a poem than an essay. Poetry is visceral, image-laden, and emotional. The Psalms furnish an excellent example for a novice worship leader to learn the art of corporate prayer, for they were corporate prayers—even the more individual ones.

Sensitivity to the community is essential in preparing prayers, as well as other elements of the worship service. In the same week, one person receives a promotion, while another is fired. A woman and her husband of fifty-three years celebrate an anniversary, while another goes to her final divorce hearing. One of the challenges of worship is to allow variety and diversity to meet these differing circumstances.

To do so requires two things of leaders in the conversation. First, they must be attentive to the congregation. They must have eyes and ears to know what is hurting and what is happening to these people who file in faithfully each Sunday. Second, worship leaders must be able to script worship in such a way that takes into account the diversity among the participants. Individuals do not worship in the same way, even within the same congregation. Personality types, diverse backgrounds, educational levels, and many other factors make it essential that worship not be scripted for only one segment of the congregation.

Koinonia (Community)

"*Koinonia,*" as preachers have solemnly told their congregations, "is the Greek word for fellowship." No word is subjected to as many misinterpretations as this one in a church. *Koinonia* simply means "common," but it is deeper in the Christian tradition than agreement or unanimity. The "commonness" that forms the basis of Christian community is the confession its members share about Jesus Christ. All of the forms of *koinonia* that live out in their midst are rooted in this foundation.

At heart, the experience of *koinonia* is about "being with" one another. We sometimes feel the need to help this with gestures, gimmicks, and forced interaction. Passing the peace is one traditional way this is done, and it takes many forms in congregations. Shared experience of worship, however, *is* "*koinonia* building." Week in and week out, as people naturally come to a regular place of worship, they cease their going, come aside, and dwell together. They experience the same script of worship, the same sermon, and the same music. They sing the same hymns.

Silence, too, has a corporate dimension. Sitting in stillness in the presence of others and praying is a different form of silence than solitude. Not all *koinonia* must be verbalized to be shared.

The observance of "sabbath" is also a form of *koinonia*. As people come aside and come together to cease their labors and worship God, they are able to relate "nonproductively" to one another. Worship invites them into a different pace of life, opening the possibility that they will engage in different kinds of conversations together.

Worship also is *koinonia* in the sharing of spiritual gifts. Worship is a collective effort. Worship leaders and preachers are crucial to worship, of course, but someone has utilized the gift of service to prepare the sanctuary. Visual settings, musical talents, and warm welcomes are all part of the giving of ourselves to one another in worship.

Sometimes people are in crisis when they come to worship. Their faith is weak, or their life is one of defeat and discouragement. The writer of Hebrews warned early Christians not to neglect "to meet together, as is the habit of some, but encouraging one another" (Heb 10:25). The very act of gathering is an act of mutual encouragement. We allow ourselves into the presence of others. We leave behind our solitary troubles and connect with like-minded believers. We cannot overestimate the power of this fellowship.

Another dimension of *koinonia* is recognition. Acknowledging one another may seem less spiritual than some concerns, but it is not. In African-American churches a long heritage exists of recognition and affirmation of individuals for leadership. In the post-Civil-War period, this was often the only place where leadership development took place.

Individuals are often lost in our society. The church, above all, ought to be that place where a sparrow's fall is noted. Simple acknowledgement is at least a form of that recognition.

Recognition also takes the form of ordination. Ordination is affirmation in the deepest sense of that word. The church publicly confirms the gifts and call of God in another and "calls them out" to go and serve on its behalf.

Worship, too, attempts to provide ways for sinful human beings to respond with repentance for their sins and brokenness. Worship is a place where confession—and restoration—rightly have a place. One of the dimensions of confession is, of course, making right our relationship with God. Another aspect of confession of sin, though, is bringing us into reconciliation with one another. It is a means of restoration to community. We end the silence and hostility of alienation and "speak to one another" again.

Even today there are many inappropriate ways in which public confession of sin takes place—what is to be confessed to God and what to others? When Dietrich Bonhoeffer wrote *Life Together*, he devoted a chapter to this very concern, perhaps anticipating the profound disintegration that would characterize the modern era. Confession was absolutely essential if a group of Christians were ever to achieve real community. Confession moves us to greater honesty and humility with one another. This confession did not, however, have to be public. When we confess to even one other Christian, Bonhoeffer wrote, we have confessed to the church.[11] In this time, the need that distresses our churches is not for public humiliation and catharsis so much as for genuine community. The point of discipline is not punishment but reclamation.

In worship, we can model and structure spaces for silent confession and public articulation of our sins through litanies and prayers. We can preach on confession. But the breakthroughs we so desperately need require alternative structures and settings. The intensive retreat and the small group provide such opportunities to build community at more intensive and intentional levels. As such, they may be considered extensions of the worshiping community.

Diakonia (Service)

We often refer to the worship "service" without realizing the implications of such a word, especially in these times in the United States when capitalistic categories have so overtaken the church. Even some educated and trained leaders do not seem to realize how crass our subjection to materialism has become. This is most evident when worship leaders subvert the true worship of God for pragmatic concerns of church growth (viewed only numerically).

Worship is often altered for the subtle agenda of numerical increase. "Evangelism" is the word cited for this justification, but the question must be raised: "If this is truly evangelism (proclamation of the good news), are we also willing to see individuals discipled somewhere other than in this congregation if that more adequately suits them?"

The very core of worship has been reversed in this tide of "marketing." Worshipers who were once expected to "serve God" are now themselves being served. That this is contrary to New Testament principles goes without saying.

However, it is not enough to shoot such an easy target, and others have done it more devastatingly.[12] We must state again the two forms of serving that belong to worship that is Christian: (1) the service of God and (2) serving one another.

In worship this transaction happens in nearly every aspect. One of the most concrete ways by which this is done, however, is through stewardship and giving. In this one part of worship, as much as any, the congregation expresses its priorities. In the Lord's Supper, too, serving is a dominant image.

What, finally, does it mean to "serve God"? To return to the analogy of the play, it is for the actor to deliver the lines faithfully. Perhaps this form of service is the one that is most indicative of what the entire "dialogue within the community" is about. How do our gestures, words, and intentions most adequately convey this essential stance—that we are God's servants?

To return to the book of Revelation, where this chapter began, there is another image—this time of those who have been martyred and surround the throne of God in heaven. It is said that they serve God day and night within the temple of God's presence (7:15). Service is the final destiny of those who love God, but it is willing and loving service. The danger of the human dialogue is that it will forget this end. Even our serving one another is not that some benign humanness would replace our worship, but that we might emulate, when we pass an offering plate or share the communion tray or affirm a young teenager's baptism, that we were made for something greater than ourselves.

Notes

[1]Maria Harris, *Fashion Me a People: Curriculum in the Church* (Louisville: Westminster/John Knox Press, 1989).

[2]While Harris lists these in order as *koinonia, leitourgia, didache, kerygma,* and *diakonia,* we will follow the order found in Gabriel Fackre's *The Christian Story: A Narrative Interpretation of Basic Christian Doctrine,* rev. ed. (Grand Rapids: Wm. B. Eerdmans Publishing Co., 1984). Fackre follows the order as listed and discussed in this chapter, placing priority on the gospel rather than the community, as Harris does. He combines *kerygma* and *didache,* differing from C. H. Dodd and others who distinguished between the two. This order emphasizes, as does this book, that worship is a response that originates with God's prior action.

[3]Suzanne Johnson, *Christian Spiritual Formation in the Church and Classroom* (Nashville: Abingdon Press, 1989) 132-35.

[4]Ibid., 132.

[5]Ibid., 134.

[6]Erik Routley, *The Divine Formula* (Princeton NJ: Prestige Publications, 1986) 20-21.

[7]See Hans von Campenhausen, *The Formation of the Christian Bible* (Philadelphia: Fortress Press, 1972).

[8]Jim McClendon has set forth a "conversionist spirituality" that embodies a full understanding of the process by which people move from "outside the faith" to "inside" in the free church understanding. He sees four phases in the spiritual life: spiritual formation (training and preparation that lead up to conversion), conversion, discipleship (growth in the faith after conversion), and what he calls the "anastatic," the unpredictable work of the Holy Spirit in a life. See James Wm. McClendon, Jr., "Toward a Conversionist Spirituality," in Gary Furr and Curtis Freeman, eds., *Ties That Bind: Life Together in the Baptist Vision* (Macon GA: Smyth & Helwys Publishing, Inc., 1994) 23-32.

[9]See C. H. Dodd, *The Apostolic Preaching and Its Development* (New York: Harper & Brothers, [1936] 1954).

[10]Fred Craddock, *Preaching* (Nashville: Abingdon Press, 1985) 70, 75.

[11]Dietrich Bonhoeffer, *Life Together: A Discussion of Christian Fellowship* (San Francisco: Harper & Row Publishers, 1954) 113.

[12]See Michael Mauldin and Edward Gilbreath, "Selling Out the House of God? Bill Hybels Answers Critics of the Seeker-Church Movement," *Christianity Today,* 18 July 1994, 20-25; Ralph C. Wood,

"The Fallacy of 'Getting Something' Out of Worship," *The Christian Ministry*, March-April 1997, 16-18; Gregory A. Pritchard, *Willow Creek Seeker Services: Evaluating a New Way of Doing Church* (Grand Rapids: Baker Books, 1996). Paul Basden offers a framework for understanding some contemporary trends in Baptist worship in " 'Something Old, Something New': Worship Styles for Baptists in the Nineties," in *Ties That Bind: Life Together in the Baptist Vision*, ed. Gary A. Furr and Curtis W. Freeman (Macon GA: Smyth & Helwys Publishing, Inc., 1994). See also Marva Dawn, *Reaching Out Without Dumbing Down* (Grand Rapids: Wm. B. Eerdmans Publishing Co., 1995).

Chapter 3
Music in the Dialogue of Worship

Milburn Price

Writing more than half a century ago in *Music and Worship*, Joseph N. Ashton identified what he perceived to be several misconceptions concerning the role of music in worship. Among the misconceptions—or misuses—cited by Ashton were:

- "a matter of traditional routine"
- a preliminary to the "main event" (the sermon) that serves primarily as "a general emotional warming up"
- an attraction related more to church advertising than to worship
- "a vehicle for individual display or group exhibition"
- a matter of aesthetic or cultural display left primarily in the hands of a group of affluent church members who serve as its patrons.[1]

It is unfortunate that, five decades later, vestiges of these misconceptions can still be observed in some settings.

To these misconceptions/misuses of music in worship, another has been added in recent years—music as entertainment. The twin influences of popular culture and commercialization have been powerful at this point (though we should acknowledge that experiencing music as entertainment is not limited to the popular-influenced genres). The related emphases of enjoying music *primarily* as sensory delight (with its related emotional stimuli) and experiencing music from a passive spectator mode have combined to create an approach to music in worship that can be observed too frequently and that undermines its potential for more effective utilization.

Given the continuing existence of both misconceptions and misuses, what *is* the proper role for music in worship? Based upon the principles presented in the preceding two chapters, I would suggest the following: *The primary functions of music in worship are to facilitate the dialogue of worship and to contribute to that dialogue.* Such an emphasis does not negate subsidiary aspects. However, it does assign primacy to the role of music in enabling worship itself to fulfill its intended purposes. This understanding forms at least part of the reason Donald Hustad refers to church music as "a functional art."[2] In those settings in which the partnering relationship between music and the dialogic structure of worship is accepted, each musical element in the worship service should be evaluated for its contribution to one facet of the dialogue: revelation, response, or conversation among the worshipers.

Revelation Through Music

The two recurring elements in the dialogue between the worshiping community and God are revelation and response. In a general sense, to the extent that music, as an aesthetic expression, both reflects and participates in the manifestation of God's creative work, it, in itself, can be viewed as a vehicle for revelation—even apart from textual associations. Thus, Karl Barth could find theological significance, as well as aesthetic delight, in the music of Mozart.[3] In a more direct sense, however, music at the service of, and in the context of, worship can contribute revelatory dimensions to the experience.

Instrumental Music

It is customary in many worshiping communities for the service to begin with instrumental music. It may be celebrative or reflective. It may be simple (a solo by guitar or other unaccompanied instrument) or elaborate (full orchestra or pipe organ with expansive tonal resources). Whatever its character or level of complexity, its purpose should be to usher the worshipers into a sense of the presence of God. Similarly, instrumental music played within the service (offertory, voluntary, or music for meditation) should contribute to the dialogue.

One possible role of instrumental music in this regard is the provision of an aural environment conducive to meditation and reflection. It offers "silence" from verbalization, though not from all sound. Harold Best suggests that "preludes, interludes, and postludes could be . . . co-offered in silence by the congregation."[4] Through the prompting of the music—and through the elimination of external noises of distraction—the worshiper is enabled to focus upon worship and to anticipate a sense of the presence of God's Spirit.

A more intentionally proactive contribution to the dialogue can occur when the instrumentalist(s) play(s) music with textual associations.[5] Of course, those associations could contribute to either revelatory or responsive elements of the dialogue. In the former case, texts that prompt the worshiper to reflect upon attributes of God or the presence of God would be particularly suitable. Notes in the worship guide (for example, "see the text of hymn ___") can make the connection explicit and further enhance the effective use of such pieces.

Vocal Music

Contributing even more directly to the process of revelation in worship is texted music (solo, ensemble, choral, or congregational) that presents "the Word of the Lord." Because vocal music presentations are at times beset by the misuses enumerated earlier in this chapter, their revelatory possibilities are too often diminished. Solos in which the primary goal of the singer seems to be either entertainment or virtuosic vocal display fail to achieve their higher purpose. Similarly, vocal ensemble or choral selections that have little relevance to the flow and structure of the worship service fall short of their potential. Such music can, however, be particularly effective when biblical texts or profound texts by "prophets" from succeeding generations, set to music that complements and gives life to the textual ideas, are given persuasive presentation by singers sensitive to their role as conveyers of the Word—at strategic places within the worship service where such a presentation logically fits. The potential usefulness of sung scripture to communicate effectively was recognized by the United Reformed Church in England and Wales when it included in its Notes concerning the Order of Worship for the Lord's Day the following: "If it [an anthem] is a Scripture passage set to music it may even on occasion serve as a substitute for one of the readings."[6]

Congregational Song

The primary role of congregational song in worship is generally considered to be that of response. However, there is a sense in which the use of well-written, theologically rich texts for congregational singing not only allows the expression of faith, but also contributes to forming the content of that faith. An autobiographical passage included by Karl Barth in his *Church Dogmatics* is illustrative:

> This [a collection of songs for children] was the text-book in which . . . I received my first theological instruction in a form appropriate to my then immaturity. And what made an indelible impression on me was the homely naturalness with which these very modest compositions spoke of the events of Christmas, Palm Sunday, Good Friday, Easter, the Ascension and Pentecost . . . For as these songs were sung in the everyday language we were then beginning to hear and speak, and as we joined in singing, we took our mother's hand, as it were, and went to the stall at Bethlehem, and to the streets of Jerusalem where, greeted by children of a similar age, the Savior made His entry, and to the dark hill of Golgotha, and as the sun rose to the garden of Joseph. . . . Yes, it was very naive, but perhaps in the very naivety [sic] there lay the deepest wisdom and greatest power.[7]

The use of song as a vehicle for conveying the Word of God has biblical precedent. It comes from a vignette near the end of the Israelite wandering in the wilderness. Moses and Joshua were summoned to the Tent of Meeting to receive final instructions from God before Moses was to relinquish leadership prior to the

Israelite entry into Canaan. On this occasion there was a preface to the instruction that was to be relayed to the people: "Write this song, and teach it to the Israelites; put it in their mouths, in order that the song may be a witness for me" (Deut 31:19). In the first forty-three verses of the following chapter is recorded the revelation that was provided—in song—for God's people at that strategic time in their pilgrimage. (Perhaps this is the origin of the term, "message in song," which is used in some church bulletins to designate the noncongregational vocal music of the day!)

For many believers—and even communities of faith—congregational song has played an important role in shaping the content of faith and in facilitating the remembering of that faith. It has been a recurring testimony that in times of sorrow, crisis, or need, assurance and comfort have come more from remembered fragments of hymn texts than from remembered words of scripture. In attempting to explain this phenomenon, Robert Mitchell suggests that the "devices of rhyme and meter and melody serve to lodge Christian truth deeply within a person's life."[8] Songs of faith offer word pictures, metaphors, and similes—as well as declarative statements—to assist in the learning and remembering process. As Paul Schilling noted, the "cumulative power of repetition" is an important factor in this process.[9]

Another insight has come from scientific studies of the hemispherical functioning of the human brain.[10] We are bipolar thinkers and learners. When the left hemisphere is dominant, our thought processes function verbally, analytically, and logically. Within the realm of right-brain activity are the intuitive, holistic aspects of thinking, including a sensitivity to overall pattern and form.

This "unity in duality" aspect of mental activity has implications for the ways in which we learn—or receive revelation—through hymn singing. Hymnic language itself is at times propositional, at times metaphorical, and at still other times a mixture of the two in varying combinations. In the preface to *What Language Shall I Borrow?* Brian Wren provided a commentary on his own creative process that is illustrative:

As a hymn-poet, I cross and recross bridges between metaphor and abstraction, the rational and the intuitive, and experience the writing of a hymn-poem as a partnership between them.[11]

Although some hymn texts do, indeed, reflect the kind of blending indicated by Wren, others communicate in primarily propositional terms. Consider, for example, "God Has Spoken by the Prophets" by George Briggs. The line of thought in this text is developed logically, leading the mind along a carefully charted path. The first stanza will serve as an example:

> God has spoken by the prophets,
> spoken the unchanging Word;
> each from age to age proclaiming,
> God the one, the righteous Lord!
> 'Mid the world's despair and turmoil
> one firm anchor holding fast:
> God eternal reigns forever,
> God the first and God the last.[12]

The hymn poem continues, still with carefully chosen language, to develop a Trinitarian understanding of the fullness of the Godhead and concludes, using a device of formal unity, with a repetition of the last line of the first stanza. The text is propositional. It is carefully constructed. It has logical development and formal unity. As a text, it represents left-brain orientation admirably.

On the other hand, consider Jaroslav Vajda's evocative "Now the Silence." Note the differences in the structure and flow of text and in the presentation of ideas:

Now the silence
Now the peace
Now the empty hands uplifted

Now the kneeling
Now the plea
Now the Father's arms in welcome

Now the hearing
Now the pow'r
Now the vessel brimmed for pouring

Now the Body
Now the Blood
Now the joyful celebration

Now the wedding
Now the songs
Now the heart forgiven leaping

Now the Spirit's visitation
Now the Son's epiphany
Now the Father's blessing

Now Now Now[13]

If you take only the words that appear in this text, it is incomplete. But the author expects the singer to bring intuitive response to the act of singing, for it helps to make the connections—to bridge the gaps left by incomplete sentence construction. In the absence of complete information, the evocation of a holistic response provides interpretive insight. Even the punctuation—or, to be more precise, the absence of punctuation—emphasizes the "stream of consciousness" character of the poetry. Thus, Vajda has provided a hymn text that appeals to right-brain understanding. For communication—or revelation—to take place, the singer must use creative thought to look beyond the words to find the reality toward which the words point.

Each kind of text—as well as mixtures of the two—offers the possibility of revelation within the act of singing.

Response Through Music

The most obvious musical vehicle through which worshipers can respond to God is congregational song. Indeed, it was its ability to enable sixteenth century believers to express themselves directly to God, without the necessity of mediation through another person, that made the hymn a powerful symbol of the Reformation doctrine of the priesthood of the believer. It has been suggested that it was the *practice* of hymn singing—as much as or even more than any of the texts that were sung—that symbolized and expressed that doctrine. In today's wide range of worship practices, worshipers sing their responses to God in traditional hymns, gospel songs, African-American spirituals, songs from the global community, contemporary Christian songs, and short choruses.

Congregational song allows worshipers to express the full range of responses discussed in chapter 1. The following list, which includes materials from differing genres of congregational song, is illustrative:

Praise
"All Glory, Laud, and Honor" (Theodulph of Orleans)
"Holy, Holy, Holy" (Reginald Heber)
"How Majestic Is Your Name" (Michael W. Smith)

Confession of Sin
"Dear Lord and Father of Mankind" (John Greenleaf Whittier)
"No, Not Despairingly" (Horatius Bonar)
"Whiter than Snow" (James Nicholson)

Thanksgiving
"For the Fruit of All Creation" (Fred Pratt Green)
"Now Thank We All Our God" (Martin Rinkart)
"Give Thanks" (Henry Smith)

Offering
"Because I Have Been Given Much" (Grace Noll Crowell)
"Take My Life and Let It Be" (Frances R. Havergal)
"We Give Thee But Thine Own" (William W. How)

Petition/Intercession
"Hope of the World" (Georgia Harkness)
"Precious Lord, Take My Hand" (Thomas A. Dorsey)
"We Utter Our Cry" (Fred Kaan)

If a concluding hymn is to serve as an authentic response to the Word of God, as it has been proclaimed through scripture, sermon, and song in that particular service—and, in doing so, to contribute to the process of spiritual formation—its textual content must be selected with care. The hymn should allow the worshiper(s) to verbalize an appropriate connection between "hearing the Word" and doing or being. For example, as the hymn of response at the conclusion of a service in which attention had been given to the sin of pride (in a sermon series on the "Seven Deadly Sins"), I selected Isaac Watts' "When I Survey the Wondrous Cross," primarily because of the first two stanzas:

> When I survey the wondrous cross,
> On which the Prince of glory died,
> My richest gain I count but loss,
> And pour contempt on all my pride.
>
> Forbid it, Lord, that I should boast,
> Save in the death of Christ, my God;
> All the vain things that charm me most,
> I sacrifice them to His blood.

Those words, as well as the climactic fourth stanza, with its all-encompassing expression of commitment, facilitated a distinctively appropriate congregational response on that occasion. Though congregational song serves as the primary musical vehicle for response in worship, its role in that regard is not exclusive. Texts expressing the various themes of response, when sung by soloists, ensembles, or choirs, provide those singers with opportunities to respond to God's revelation. At the same time, however, the congregation can vicariously participate in that response *if their attention is drawn to the responsive nature and intended function of those texts.* (Printing the texts in the worship guide may facilitate this sense of vicarious participation.) Developing a congregational sensitivity to such an understanding of their participatory role during solo, ensemble, or choral music is one of the functions of worship planning and leadership.

There is another understanding of response for both vocal and instrumental musicians who "perform" during a worship service. If biblical teachings about stewardship are applied in a holistic sense, the "performance" of music within the context of worship can be viewed as an offering—an act of faithful stewardship of musical gifts. For the musicians, the music that is performed becomes their offering—the "fruit" resulting from the sustained, disciplined work that is required for the development of musical skills and for their application to a particular piece of music.

Music in the Congregational Dialogue

Just as music can facilitate and contribute to the dialogue between the worshiper and God, it can function in similar fashion in the dialogue within the worshiping community. In a general sense, the act of congregational singing—when engaged in purposefully— helps to form a sense of community (*koinonia*). The uniting of voices (and accompanying instruments) enables a worshiping body to express shared beliefs about God and shared responses to God *as a community.* In more specific ways texted music gives voice to some of the recurring themes of the congregational dialogue.

Confession of Faith

For centuries congregations have sung or heard sung affirmations of faith that have served as core beliefs of the community. Since the Credo was incorporated into the Roman Mass in 1014,[14] musical settings of that statement of faith (the Niceno-Constantinopolitan Creed) enabled its tenets to be affirmed by worshiping congregations through succeeding centuries. In the Catholic worship tradition—until the reforms of the Second Vatican Council—it was customarily sung by either priest (in chant) or choir on behalf of the gathered community. Sixteenth-century German congregations who followed Martin Luther's reforms often sang *"Wir glauben all an einen Gott,"* Luther's free translation of the Nicene Creed, following the sermon. Musical settings of this text for both choir and congregation continue to be sung by worshiping communities today, particularly in those churches following liturgical worship patterns.

For evangelical churches, the primary vehicle for singing about the content of faith has been the hymn. Those hymns that frame responses to God—hymns of praise, confession, thanksgiving, petition, and commitment—inevitably contain or imply elements of faith content. However, there are other hymns whose texts are specifically intended to enable the congregation to "speak to one another" and to affirm to each other what they believe. Martin Luther's *"Ein' feste Burg,"* which we know through Frederick Hedge's translation as "A Mighty Fortress Is Our God," is such a hymn. The direction of communication is not *to* God; the text is *about* God. Thus, the congregation reminds itself through its singing of the strong foundation of its faith in God through Jesus Christ.

A more recent hymn by Fred Pratt Green also serves the need for congregations to sing their faith to one another:

This is the threefold truth
On which our faith depends;
And with this joyful cry
Worship begins and ends:
Christ has died!
Christ has risen!
Christ will come again!

Made sacred by long use,
New-minted for our time,
Our liturgies sum up
The hope we have in him:
Christ has died!
Christ has risen!
Christ will come again!

On this we fix our minds
As, kneeling side by side,
We take the bread and wine
From Him, the Crucified:
Christ has died!
Christ has risen!
Christ will come again!

By this we are upheld
When doubt or grief assails
Our Christian fortitude,
And only grace avails:
Christ has died!
Christ has risen!
Christ will come again!

This is the threefold truth
Which, if we hold it fast,
Changes the world and us
And brings us home at last.
Christ has died!
Christ has risen!
Christ will come again![15]

Vocal soloists, ensembles, and choirs can also contribute to the musical confession of faith. In some instances it may be appropriate for them to sing *to* the congregation, as a reminder of important elements of belief. In other instances, however, their presentation would more appropriately be viewed as singing *on behalf of* the congregation.

Exhortation and Encouragement

Through song the gathered community often finds a fruitful way to fulfill in the present day Paul's twin admonitions to the Hebrews to "provoke one another to love and good deeds" and to "encourage one another" (Heb 10:24-25). These sung congregational exhortations and words of encouragement take a variety of emphases.

- They gather the congregation for *worship*.
  ("Brethren [Christians], We Have Met to Worship")
- They call the community to sing *praise* to God.
  ("Come, Christians, Join to Sing")
  ("Come, We that Love the Lord")
- They invite *celebration* in festive seasons of the Christian year.
  ("Good Christians, All Rejoice")
- They call sinners to *repentance*.
  ("Come, Ye Sinners, Poor and Needy")
- They offer *comfort* in times of sorrow or discouragement.
  ("Come, Ye Disconsolate")
  ("If You Will Only Let God Guide You")
- They urge faithful *service*—or *diakonia*.
  ("Come, All Christians, Be Committed")

Soloists, ensembles, and choirs can likewise participate in the dialogue within the community by singing either settings of appropriate hymn texts, such as those mentioned above, or other selections that offer exhortation ("Find Us Faithful" and "Beloved, Let Us Love One Another"), encouragement ("I Lift Mine Eyes unto the Hills"), or a combination of both ("Be Strong in the Lord").

Musical Styles as "Dialects"

Travelers to a country in which the prevailing language differs from their own often find dialogue difficult, unless they have developed proficiency in speaking and understanding that language. Even within some languages, differences in dialects serve as further barriers to clarity of communication.

In recent years divisive tensions have developed in many worshiping communities over the issue of which musical styles should be utilized. The issue is complicated because for many people musical styles tend to function as "dialects." They are more "comfortable" with musical styles with which they are familiar and they like. It is true that, whereas a person's linguistic dialect is shaped primarily by cultural environment, that same person's taste in musical styles is shaped by both cultural environment and personal preference. The barriers to clear communication are no less obtrusive, however, even though they may be more psychological than linguistic.

When a congregation is confronted with conflicting views concerning musical styles that should be used in their worship, it may be helpful to approach the issue from the perspective of musical style as an analogy to speech dialect. What musical style forms the prevailing (preferred?) dialect for that particular congregation? Are there multiple musical styles ("dialects") represented by the preferences of significant numbers of congregation members? The likelihood of such diversity increases as the size and heterogeneity of a church expand.

Though not himself a musician, C. S. Lewis offered a solution to such tensions over musical styles in his essay "On Church Music."[16] In addressing tensions between musical "High Brows" and "Low Brows" in British churches, he suggested that tolerance and mutual deference provide a "means of grace" and that "discrepancies of taste and capacity will, indeed, provide matter for mutual charity and humility."[17]

There is considerable merit in this approach. In some settings it may, indeed, work. Where a conflicted congregation can agree to be "bilingual" or "multilingual" in the acceptance of musical styles, it may be possible for a diversity of musical styles to coexist. In such cases, each musical faction experiences great satisfaction when the "dialogue" of worship features its preferred "musical dialect," and either learns to be "multilingual" by cultivating an understanding of and appreciation for other styles or, at the least, patiently endures other musical styles for the sake of the community.

On the other hand, there exist those congregations in which preference for a single musical style (or perhaps a combination of two compatible styles) is so securely established that the corporate personality of the congregation is closely linked to it. For these congregations, the preferred musical "dialect" may range from traditional to "contemporary." In such instances, it may be appropriate for that body of believers to be true to its own sense of identify, to focus its musical attention in worship upon its preferred "dialect," and to welcome into its community those persons who may be attracted to such a well-defined identity.

The answers to this issue are not easy ones, in spite of recent efforts by church growth specialists to prescribe a single musical model for all churches that would aspire to growth. The implication in a recent book on church growth that the *only* growing churches are those in which music "is contemporary and upbeat"[18] ignores evidence to the contrary. Although demographics have, indeed, contributed to a recent phenomenon in which a large number of churches—particularly in urban areas—that use "contemporary and upbeat" music have grown rapidly, there are other congregations that have experienced steady growth while consciously avoiding the rejection of past musical traditions and the unquestioning embrace of music influenced strongly by popular culture—particularly rock music.

A "neighborly" (and humble) approach for a congregation establishing its stylistic identity would lead it to be honest with itself—and true to its own sense of calling as a worshiping community. Then, once crucial decisions concerning approach have been made, they should be implemented without attributing *spiritual* superiority to the musical style(s) chosen!

Notes

[1]Joseph N. Ashton, *Music in Worship* (Boston/Chicago: The Pilgrim Press, 1943) 1-5.

[2]Donald P. Hustad, *Jubilate II: Church Music in Worship and Renewal* (Carol Stream IL: Hope Publishing Company, 1993) 22 ff.

[3]See Karl Barth, *Wolfgang Amadeus Mozart*, trans. Clarence K. Pott (Grand Rapids: Wm. B. Eerdmans Publishing Co., 1986).

[4]Harold M. Best, *Music Through the Eyes of Faith* (San Francisco: HarperCollins Publishers, 1993) 197.

[5]Robert H. Mitchell discusses this use as "worship through ideas" in *Ministry and Music* (Philadelphia: The Westminster Press, 1978) 71.

[6]Quoted in Erik Routley, *The Divine Formula* (Princeton NJ: Prestige Publications, 1986) 125-26.

[7]Karl Barth, *The Doctrine of Reconciliation*, vol. 4, pt. 2 of *Church Dogmatics*, trans. G. W. Bromiley (Edinburgh: T. & T. Clark, 1958) 112-13.

[8]Mitchell, 80.

[9]For a more extended discussion of this matter, see S. Paul Schilling, *The Faith We Sing* (Philadelphia: The Westminster Press, 1983) 23-28.

[10]For an informative survey of research concerning hemispheric differences in the brain, see Sally P. Springer and Georg Deutsch, *Left Brain, Right Brain*, 3rd ed. (New York: W. H. Freeman and Company, 1989). Particularly relevant to the assumptions made in this chapter concerning the functioning of different types of hymns in the learning and remembering process are pages 283-87.

[11]Brian Wren, *What Language Shall I Borrow?* (New York: Crossroad Publishing Company, 1989) 5.

[12]George Wallace Briggs, "God Has Spoken by the Prophets," in *Holding in Trust: Hymns of the Hymn Society in the United States and Canada* (Carol Stream IL: Hope Publishing Company, 1992) 30.

[13]Jaroslav J. Vajda, "Now the Silence," in *Now the Joyful Celebration* (St. Louis: Morning Star Music Publishers) 39.

[14]Don Michael Randel, ed., *The New Harvard Dictionary of Music* (Cambridge MA: The Belknap Press of Harvard University Press, 1986) 212.

[15]Fred Pratt Green, *The Hymns and Ballads of Fred Pratt Green* (Carol Stream IL: Hope Publishing Company, 1982) 96-97.

[16]C. S. Lewis, "On Church Music," in *Christian Reflections*, ed. Walter Hooper (Grand Rapids: Wm. B. Eerdmans Publishing Co., 1967) 94-99.

[17]Ibid., 97.

[18]James Emery White, *Opening the Front Door: Worship and Church Growth* (Nashville: Convention Press, 1992) 83.

Chapter 4

Worship Planning

Connecting the Conversations

Gary Furr and Milburn Price

For the weekly dialogue of worship that takes place in a particular community of believers to maintain a sense of vitality and purposefulness, it is important for the conversations within the context of worship to be preceded and prepared by a series of conversations among the worship leaders. The size and organizational structure of a congregation will determine the number of persons who should participate in these planning conversations. Except for those very small communities of faith in which the pastor alone prepares the sermon and order of worship, including the selection of hymns (presumably in the absence of even a part-time minister of music), the planning team should include, at a minimum, the pastor and minister of music (whether part-time or full-time).

Preliminary planning conversations for a given worship service should begin several weeks in advance. It is important for the church musician to know sermon topics and scripture readings sufficiently far in advance to be able to select solo, ensemble, and/or choral music appropriate for the occasion and to allow adequate time for rehearsal preparation. Such advance notice also allows time for teaching to the congregation a new hymn that might be particularly appropriate. (The kind of intentional coordination of the dialogue of worship envisioned by the principles presented in earlier chapters is difficult at best—and in most instances impossible—when sermon topics are determined only a few days in advance!) Periodic conversations devoted to long-range planning of major worship emphases (observance of seasons of the Christian year or a thematic series of sermons, for example) provide good starting points for worship planning.

The week prior to the worship event calls for focused conversations devoted to developing structure for the service, arranging its constituent elements in a manner that facilitates the dialogue, and providing both connectedness and relatedness among those elements. In some settings all of these things may be accomplished in one extended worship planning session. In other situations the planning process may proceed through a series of shorter conversations that allow for a creative interplay of conversation and reflection. ("After our recent conversation, I thought of a more appropriate hymn of response following the sermon," or "What if we used this responsive reading I just found as a vehicle for congregational confession?")

Whatever form or style the planning conversations take, a combination of both long-range and short-term communication will be helpful to provide the most thoughtful and intentional planning for worship.

Structures

In any given worship service, the varied elements (scripture readings, hymns, prayers, sermon, anthem, and perhaps others) are combined, either intentionally or unintentionally, into some sequence that creates a structure, or form. Robert H. Mitchell has identified four types of worship structure.[1]

The first type, the "variety" model, reflects an absence of thoughtful planning and, thus, is not relevant to the task of providing meaningful planning to connect the strands of conversation that form the dialogue of worship. As Mitchell describes his "variety" model,

> Each item stands alone. . . . Its primary characteristic is that there is no visible rational basis for organization other than the principle of variety and the fact that everything is somehow related to God.[2]

He later refers to this model as "a Christian variety show" in which worship planners work independently of each other, with no attempt to coordinate or relate the various worship elements to each other. Obviously, this approach is an example of "non-planning" that is antithetical to the assumptions about worship planning that form the foundation for this chapter. (Note, Mitchell acknowledges its faults and presents it descriptively as an approach he has observed, not one he would advocate.) Nonetheless, because this approach can, indeed, be observed in the worship practices of some churches, it is presented here as an example of a faulty model that calls for revision/correction. However, each of Mitchell's other three types has relevance to the creation of structures of worship in a dialogical mode and will be discussed in that light.

The Thematic Model

In Mitchell's thematic model all of the elements of the worship service "have a common focus." Each service is constructed so that it develops a single theme through the coordinated focus of scripture, sermon, hymns, solo, readings, and anthem.[3]

The use of a thematic model has the seeming advantage of facilitating worship planning by providing a single "topic" around which the conversations of worship will be developed on a particular day. It is, in some instances, possible to construct a meaningful dialogue around some themes that offer multifaceted possibilities for development. This approach is particularly useful for special observances of the Christian year such as Christmas, Easter, and Pentecost; for broadly stated themes such as God's grace, God's love, or the church; and for special worship occasions such as a wedding or a funeral. The more specifically defined the occasion, the more useful the thematic approach will be.

However, potential difficulties become immediately apparent when considering this model for implementation on a week-by-week basis. Difficulty in finding suitable materials for *every* component of the service increases as the theme becomes more sharply defined. Of even greater seriousness is the absence of that openness of conversation that allows for the meeting of the diverse concerns and needs of the gathered community. Furthermore, except for broadly interpreted themes, this model does not lend

itself easily to addressing the multiple forms of response to God
identified in chapter 1.

The Alternation Model

The alternation model, based upon the Isaiah 6 passage discussed
earlier, has been the basis for traditional liturgical structures of
worship. Mitchell's description of it recalls the pattern of dialogical interaction that has been discussed recurringly in this book:
"The Creator is seen and the creature responds; God calls and
man [sic] answers."[4]

At first thought, this model would seem to be an optimum
structure to implement the understanding of worship we have
been discussing. Its construction emulates a dialogical pattern that
provides alternation in the direction of conversation between God
and the worshipers. It allows for the incorporation of both the
presentation of the Word of God to the gathered community and
varied responses (praise, confession, thanksgiving, and renewed
commitment) from the worshipers.

Mitchell expresses one concern about this model:

> Functionally, a liturgy that is organized this way almost requires,
> by its very nature, the participation of a priestly figure—one
> who speaks to God on behalf of the people and, more impor-
> tantly, one who speaks as the voice of God in asking the
> searching question, pronouncing the absolution, and calling to
> commitment.[5]

Of course, such a conclusion depends upon one's theological
perspective—who is/can be a "priest." This concern, it seems, is
minimized in settings in which varied means are used to convey
both the Word of God (scripture, sermon, anthem, drama) and the
response of the people (congregational prayers, hymns, responsive
readings).

There is, however, another substantive concern. In its strictest
application, the alternation model restricts the dialogue to inter-
changes between God and the worshipers. There is no place for

the various aspects of dialogue within the community as discussed in chapter 2. On the other hand, the alternation model does emphasize the fact that the conversation between the worshipers and God is the *primary* one.

The Conversational Model

Mitchell's conversational model of worship structure would also seem to fit well with the analogy of worship as dialogue. Indeed, he suggests that the flow of worship is patterned after informal, small-group worship experiences that develop "conversationally" —that is, one idea leads to another, even though the latter idea may take the conversation in a different direction. The distinguishing structure of this model is that "a variety of things may be experienced, but each of them will have a specific purposefulness *that grows out of the preceding event.*"[6]

There is great flexibility with this model. That flexibility allows the inclusion of a variety of types of both revelation and response (as in the alternation model), without insisting that the dialogue alternate with any specific regularity between the worshiper and God. It also opens the possibility—even the probability—of dialogue within the community. It is not theme-bound, but creates space for a multiplicity of themes—if they are connected and interwoven purposefully. All elements of the worship service (*even the sermon*—if there is one) are flexible in their placement within the structure.

There are, however, difficulties inherent with this approach to worship structure. Planning is time intensive, because each service begins anew. It is an idea in search of a new embodiment each week. The planning conversations required to create the weekly worship conversations require significant time investment on the part of worship leaders each week, and this model almost presupposes implementation in a group of worshipers homogenous enough for worship planners to anticipate congregational reaction to the unfolding of events.

Further, careful attention must be given to providing a connectedness to the dialogue. Worship planners and leaders must strategize carefully the ways in which transitions will lead naturally and logically from one emphasis to another. Care also must be given to distinguishing among the various "directions" of the conversation (God's Word addresses worshipers, worshipers respond to God, worshipers speak to each other).

A Dialogic Model

Any one of Mitchell's latter three models can serve as a suitable structure for the framing of a worship service based upon the principles established for worship as dialogue. Each model presents difficulties to be overcome, however.

As an alternative to the exclusive use of any one of these models, a hybrid model that combines the most desirable characteristics of either two or all three of Mitchell's models, while maintaining the principles of "worship as dialogue," might be considered. That approach, which we will call a "dialogic model," could be flexible, allowing subtle nuances of structure from week to week. For example, within a worship service structured primarily along the alternation model, there might be an extended section devoted to the presentation of the Word of God that provided a thematic emphasis (through convergence of scripture, solo or anthem, and sermon). Another possibility would be the shaping of a service in the conversational model to provide some of the differing emphases of the alternation model. Even a service planned primarily in accordance with the thematic model could be allowed the freedom to introduce elements of confession or petition.

A primary value of the dialogic model would be its allowance for openness and diversity in planning from week to week, under the leadership of God's Spirit. For most congregations, radical changes in structure on a weekly basis are unsettling. However, a worship planning team could determine a *primary* structure as a point of beginning for the weekly worship planning cycle and allow the concept of the hybrid model to provide subtle differences to that primary structure on a weekly basis.

Whatever the structure chosen, faithfulness to the concept of dialogue is crucial for worship to be participatory rather than passive.

"Tossing and Catching"

The preceding discussion of structures for worship presupposes that, for the weekly conversations taking place when the community gathers for worship to have significant meaning on a recurring basis, they must have a sense of both purposefulness and connectedness. In *The Divine Formula*, Erik Routley suggested an analogy between the conversations of worship and the process of tossing and catching a ball.[7] As used by Routley, the analogy became a device to call for creativity in thinking about and planning for worship. So how are purposefulness, connectedness, and creativity related?

Though he did not intend it precisely in this way, Routley's analogy can be connected usefully to the analogy that has served as the foundation for this book—worship as dialogue. His act of "tossing" may be considered comparable to those portions of a worship service in which God's Word is presented. "Catching" then becomes analogous to the worshipers both hearing and responding to that Word.

Much of the work of worship planners is often devoted to "tossing." What ideas will be conveyed? Through what means will the Word of God be presented to the worshipers? Who will be the "tossers"—or worship leaders?

These are not unimportant questions, but it is equally important to consider the mechanics of "tossing" and "catching." In the game of "toss and catch," it is not sufficient that the ball be thrown; the transaction is not completed until another person has caught it.

Similarly, in worship planning, it is inadequate simply to decide upon the subject matter of presentation, without considering how it may be received. In what ways can the Word of God be presented so that it connects with the worshipers' experience and understanding and has relevance to their daily lives? How can that presentation encourage an authentic, appropriate response from the worshipers? How can the varied strands of conversations be connected into a meaningful whole? How can the overall structure of the service facilitate a series of revelations and responses ("tosses" and "catches")? Responding insightfully to these questions requires a knowledge of the congregation one serves and an understanding of the foundational principles of worship.

Once the service has been planned, the work of worship leaders is not yet done. Not being mind readers, members of the congregation will not have the advantage of knowing how carefully the service has been constructed. Nor will they always sense the subtle connections that have been made to create a potentially smooth flow from one element to another. Therefore, occasional *brief* verbal links between elements may assist the dialogue. These serve as "promptings" from the worship leaders to remind worshipers of their place in the "script."

One danger in worship planning should be noted: the danger of trying to *manipulate* the response. Part of the risk of playing "toss and catch" is that the tossed ball—no matter how skillfully, carefully, or gently it is thrown—may be missed. Worship planners and leaders must humbly acknowledge that after all of the planning has been done, and after the worship service has been prayerfully and artfully led, it is the work of God's Spirit—not that of the worship leaders—to produce an appropriate response!

Notes

[1]Robert H. Mitchell, *Ministry and Music* (Philadelphia: The Westminster Press, 1978) 97-105.
[2]Ibid., 97.
[3]Ibid., 99.
[4]Ibid., 100.
[5]Ibid., 102.
[6]Ibid., 103.
[7]Erik Routley, *The Divine Formula* (Princeton: Prestige Publications, 1986). For some of the applications of this analogy, see 13-15, 37-41, 65-72.

Chapter 5

Worship in Other Settings

Gary Furr

Human communication is so pervasive that we take it for granted. Its astounding character can best be seen in a growing child as he or she crosses the threshold of language and begins to communicate. Throughout life that same child will grow up to communicate with others in a variety of ways—giving formal presentations in front of a group, talking to small groups of friends, selling a product to a customer, rebuking his or her children, and exchanging intimacies with a spouse.

The essential character of communication does not change even when its setting does. Tone of voice, volume, terms of address, and nonverbal gestures may change, but communication does not. Worship corresponds to this essential character of communication.

The Multiple Settings of Worship

The patriarchs in the book of Genesis responded to their encounters with God by creating sacred places. Abraham built an altar on the mountain after God appeared to him with the covenant promise. Isaac had a dream in the night in which God renewed the covenant of his fathers with him. There he built an altar to remember the occasion, and he worshiped the Lord. Jacob, too, after he met God at Bethel, built an altar to commemorate the place where he met God in the night when he was fleeing from Esau.[1]

Jesus touched on this same universality of worship in John 4 during his conversation with the Samaritan woman. During their conversation she raised the question of the proper place for the true worship of God. Jesus replied that "God is spirit, and those who worship him must worship in spirit and truth" (v. 24).

These two selections from the Bible point to a "trinity" of truths: (1) Worship is not limited to a certain place. (2) Worship is not confined to certain times. (3) Worship is not only a corporate experience; it may happen anytime and anywhere when a single individual responds to God's action. Such response, however well-planned or poorly-expressed, is worship when it is directed to the living God.

In worship we see the tension between two fundamental realities that are lived out in the congregation—the corporate and the individual. Worship is a dialogue, consisting of what God says, but also in how humans respond. That response takes many forms.

Don Saliers speaks of a "canon" of essential elements for Christian worship. He identifies four basic structures that have comprised the defining elements of worship in the broad Christian tradition: (1) the rites of initiation, (2) the Lord's Supper, or Communion, (3) the cycles of time, and (4) the patterns of prayer. Whatever variations Christians may display in how these are practiced, he says, they are universally present.[2]

Saliers adds a fifth element: the "pastoral" services of worship. These include marriage and funeral rites, services of penitence and reconciliation, and various forms of prayer with the sick and dying.[3] In the present context many Christians are also interested in the recovery of a place for the ministry of healing. The ritualized expression of prayer for healing could be included in this fifth category.

Worship is a dialogue that connects with all of life, not simply with the hour or so when we worship on Sunday morning. By examining some of these occasional contexts, we are able to see that worship is part of the ongoing conversation between God and a human life in all of its dimensions.

Worship as Ritual

Worship is ritual response to God. That does not mean all worship is highly formal or liturgical in expression, but worship, at even its most spontaneous demonstration, takes ritual form.

The special settings of worship emphasize the importance of ritual for worship. This concept is misunderstood because we often distinguish between ritual and spontaneity or between ritual and sincerity. These are false distinctions. All worship takes some ritual form if it ever attains any structure at all. Even silence has a structure—if the individual follows a meditation, or lights a candle as a way of entering silence, or concludes the time by saying the Lord's Prayer. Ritual may be formal or informal, structured or implicit. There are, therefore, communal rituals, but also individual rituals. Rituals can be very eccentric. We often ritualize experiences and crises that are so profound they are beyond our capacity to process without help, for example, death, marriage, and adulthood (in our society symbolized by graduation).

Theologian Paul Tillich defined a symbol as something that points beyond itself to something greater, and yet to some extent participates in that to which it points.[4] Rituals and symbols can, of course, become idolatrous. The problem is distinguishing between true and false symbols.

The question, then, is not *whether* we will have ritual in worship, but *which* ritual we will use and how faithful that ritual is to the gospel. The unreflective intermingling of symbols can sometimes confuse and hurt more than help. We may be guilty of trivialization or, worse, of co-opting the sacred for not-so-ultimate concerns.

Therefore, whenever we structure worship, we employ ritual and symbol. On some special occasions, such as weddings or funerals, or in special settings, such as the retreat, ritual will have a heightened importance. In a situation that is likely to have dynamics of unfamiliarity (the people gathered have not been together in this grouping before) or anxiety (they are negotiating a great moment of life), ritual provides the "script" for the moment. Ritual does not always refer to repetition or boredom, but it does mean that worship involves intention.

Ritual occasions function in two ways in our lives. These special occasions heighten our sense of how worship is a *connection* —with God, with others, and with ourselves. This connectedness is the essence of conversation. Dialogue is where the leap of faith takes flesh and understanding occurs. Special occasions also provide a *structure* through which we are able to give voice to our deepest yearnings and needs.

One way to think about this idea is as *prepositions* in the language. Prepositions are words of connection. They often provide the bridge between one word and some other word in the sentence. Theologically, we might think of them as the spaces where the Holy Spirit is at work. Different prepositions function in different contexts, but all have the same essential task—to make connection and help complete the sentence. So corporate worship is one type of "preposition," a solitary retreat another, but both have a similar function.

Therefore, different contexts and forms of worship function as different "prepositions," yet all in their various ways contribute to the different connections of a body of believers with God and with one another. These connections provide the dialogue of worship.

Don Saliers' categories of "times of prayer" and of "pastoral" services coincide with our interest in the various other settings in the life of a congregation in which worship takes place (or ought to take place). Because these occasions are more specialized, they have a heightened sense of "passage"; yet they demonstrate specifically what all worship does generally. They demonstrate for us how much "conversation" needs the prepositional function of worship.

With this thought in mind, we will look at various other ways we worship. While the list would go beyond what is treated here, we will consider five expressions of worship that touch on the areas of prayer and pastoral concerns: (1) "personal worship" and devotions, (2) small group and retreat settings, (3) weddings, (4) funerals, and (5) transitions.

"Personal Worship"
The Devotional Life and Corporate Worship

Some of the dialogue and connection with God happens *within* our individual lives. These are the internal experiences of God in dialogue with our particular experiences in life—voices of childhood, the accumulation of experiences we have had, and our reactions—good or bad—to them.

The preposition "within" is a good description of the function of personal prayer in the worship life of a Christian. Personal devotions and corporate worship, however, often seem to be opposites. Many people believe, artificially, that they are not connected. For some, gathering in groups to worship and pray is less fulfilling than personal and private time with God. For others, the idea of worshiping alone is difficult. They are enriched and helped by connection with the larger community.

Yet, these two are opposite ends of a single continuum where worship is concerned. On the one end is our solitude before God; at the other end is our common faith in Christ and fellowship with God that forms our fellowship with one another. They are different forms of "conversation."

It is essential that we have both dimensions of worship in our lives if we are to find healthy balance spiritually. Dietrich Bonhoeffer wrote *Life Together* as a guide for a community of faith. It has been used as a retreat guide and offers some helpful warnings and corrections to the distortions of worship and prayer that can occur. In it he writes:

> Many people seek fellowship because they are afraid to be alone. Because they cannot stand loneliness, they are driven to seek the company of other people. There are Christians, too, who cannot endure being alone, who have had some bad experiences with themselves, who hope they will gain some help in association with others. They are generally disappointed. Then they blame the fellowship for what is really their own fault. The Christian community is not a spiritual sanatorium. The person who comes

into a fellowship because he is running away from himself is misusing it for the sake of diversion, no matter how spiritual this diversion may appear.[5]

Here Bonhoeffer touches on something that is epidemic in the twentieth century—the impoverishment of selfhood. The desire to be always in the company and fellowship of others is not good for us. We need that sense of "coming and going," of gathering to praise and dispersing to serve and live, of presence and absence. One of the values in personal devotional life is the attention of the person to his or her individuality before God.

Corporate worship does not exist merely to "meet our needs," though it most certainly and often does. If we come only to meet social needs, then the eventual results are what we deserve—a fellowship based upon what we get from one another. The purpose of the individual's personal spiritual life is a healthy sense of individuality that is not free of the community so much as it is free to bring something *to* the community.

The individual journey is one that contributes finally to the larger community by spending time in attention to God and the things of God. Public worship is often populated by broken selves. It can contribute to the healing of those selves. So, too, can the personal journeys to wholeness of those selves contribute to the healing of our worshiping communities.

This healing journey is not one that arrives all at once, of course. In Galatians 4:19, Paul uses the word *morphe* when he says that in the Christian life there is travail "until Christ is *formed* in you." Here is the image of an embryo, of development and growth that takes place over time.

The zeal for social connection is not the only danger to spiritual health. Bonhoeffer wrote, "Let him who cannot be alone beware of community. Let him who is not in community beware of being alone."[6] Individualism can be as detrimental to a fellowship as overly dependent personalities.

Many people conceive of "the devotional life" as a private experience, the "quiet time" in which they are disconnected from others. While everyone needs time and space for prayer, this is not an adequate conception of that practice. The idea of "private worship," or personal devotions, is, strictly speaking, impossible. By "private worship" we actually mean that it is personal—between the individual and God. Theologically, however, this is not so. Fellowship with God is always fellowship with the saints, even when we are absolutely alone in the physical sense.

What is "prayer without ceasing"? Some interpret this to mean that we are to enter into a personal state of prayerfulness perpetually, and this is a worthy goal. Another way to think about this, however, is to see the act of prayer as the vocation of the whole church. Even when we pray alone, we are in communion with all saints of the ages.

We need the experience of solitude and prayer as well as corporate prayer. Neither is a substitute for the other. Our deficiencies in prayer are not unrelated to the problems we experience in corporate worship. We are unable to find inward quiet. We suffer from diminished attention spans and disorders. Our knowledge of the scriptures, our lack of consensus among the different versions, diversity in devotional materials, all reflect the impact of an activist, market-oriented culture.

The same unsettledness and disruption is evident in the people who comprise our churches. Some chronologically change congregations, some perpetually engage in congregational conflicts, and our fellowships are rent by disrupted families—evidences of a deeper disquiet.

Some leaders desperately try to answer these tremors by adjusting or changing forms of worship. This approach adds only one more stress in the lives of people. The only reasons adequate to change worship are theological and spiritual ones, not pragmatism, nor even to give pastoral reassurance or to achieve aesthetic excellence. One of the things we can do to run against this grain of disintegration is to connect prayer more meaningfully to the larger corporate community. Many helpful resources are available, but the same elements of good worship are also essential to prayer—the heartfelt praise of God, the reading and hearing of scripture, confession of sin, intercession and petition, and response (this can take the form of commitments we make, writing in a journal, or acts of response—such as touching a cross or lighting a candle).

The most significant shift the church could make is in teaching its members how, once again, to listen to God speaking through the Scriptures. We must again teach the Bible with depth and passion. To do so will require an investment by our members of time and energy. The individual's devotional life, worship "within," is a form of preparation for the worshiping community when it gathers.

Small Group and Retreat Settings

The small group and the retreat are gatherings of special intensity in which Christians may experience fellowship, study, and prayer in depth. The prepositional phrase "together with" comes to mind when we think of the retreat. In smaller gatherings a strong sense of belonging and intimacy can develop quickly. It is also a setting in which individuals often experience personal transformation.

The revival has been a dominant form of transformation in worship among evangelical Christians. Revivalism has a stylized form of worship, complete with musical preferences and behavioral goals (decisions for Christ). Revivalism is not dead, but its forms are not always well-suited for a highly-educated society like ours. The retreat and the small group have taken their places alongside the revival as significant occasions for spiritual growth and transformation. In the future they may even replace revivals as a primary setting for spiritual encounter outside regular weekly worship.

If that is so, then when we gather in retreats and small groups, we may be modeling transformative worship norms for the future. There are great advantages to the retreat setting. Since groups are typically smaller than congregational worship, there is mobility in the worship, flexibility, and openness to innovation. The retreat is a natural place to experiment and adapt.

This adaptation needs to be considered carefully, however. First, whatever new ideas retreatants carry back to their congregation will become part of the collective experience (and sometimes the set of expectations) of that fellowship of believers. Changes in worship patterns always require explanation and patient implementation. The retreat can be an occasion for worship education and training. Here we may introduce the broader tradition of Christian worship to people who are probably only familiar with their own particular heritage of worship. Sometimes it can be an opportunity to introduce people to their own diverse heritage.

Generally, the smaller and more informal the gathering, the simpler the worship will be. This does not mean that the worship cannot be liturgical or structured. The same elements of worship speak in this setting as on any worship occasion. In a retreat, movement and participation can be much higher. Silences can be longer or directed. Intercessory prayer and prayers of petition may be longer. The "hurry" of daily life is removed, and worship is allowed what might be its typical pace if we lived as we ought.

Even with the best of intentions, however, the fluid, unstructured nature of the retreat can lead to some collisions of tradition, preference, and theology. Like any worship occasion, the retreat should reflect careful, faithful planning and thought.

The retreat is an occasion for innovation and demonstrative worship, which may be a positive factor. It can be a time to try out different and new approaches. If we try to take this experience back to a larger body, however, we immediately encounter problems. Smaller gatherings have different dynamics than larger ones. Enthusiastic participants, emotionally stirred, can inappropriately transfer worship expectations to the larger group. This same uncritical reaction can also happen on the personal level. It is also important to avoid elitism and impatience with those who have not "experienced what we have" in a more intensive setting.

A student of Dietrich Bonhoeffer once commented that one of the callings of true community is "to keep the word from being spiritualized, individualized, and de-politicized."[7] The retreat is an intensive experience that often seems more "real" than our daily grind, full of responsibility and complexity, where emotional catharsis also can be an escape from the realities of our lives. It can be a substitute for our responsibilities in the world.

The only antidote is the sanity of genuine Christian community, where there is freedom to express, discuss, pray, and seek the truth, but also where there is an endeavor to connect these discoveries with the larger community and the world. Smaller gatherings of the church exist, not to replace the larger community, but to serve as leaven, to return to it.

In these smaller settings, the conversation of the larger community is continued in a more intimate setting, like a whispered aside between a husband and wife at a family gathering. This more personal and intimate expression of worship can feed and enhance the larger community. It can also be the occasion of misunderstanding and distance. For that reason, this "preposition" of worship should be used with sensitivity. The intimacy, informality, and intensity of the retreat will often be more attractive to some individuals than the larger corporate expression of the church, but should never become a substitute for that larger connection.

The Wedding as Worship

It may not be customary to think about a wedding as a crisis, unless one has planned one recently, but weddings, too, represent a transitional moment. The wedding marks the end of parenting and the attendant grief of that loss for parents, the beginning of adult responsibility, and the formation of a new marriage and home.

It is also a time of "covenant renewal" for the community. The church structures and bounds this set of commitments with its own story—a story of faithfulness and love demonstrated on the cross. As such, a wedding is a worship service.

The wedding embodies the realm of relationships in worship. The preposition "between" seems fitting to describe it. Like all corporate worship, it is an occasion of multiple connections and bonds. Families face their past again—the pain of divorce is expressed in the difficulties with where to seat Dad and his new wife, or two family members who have not spoken in years must now face one another. A wedding invites us to look more carefully at ourselves and our relationships with others.

It is important that the church reclaim the wedding as an extension of its worshiping dimension. For too long, church facilities have been considered as "wedding chapels" in local communities, and the church has been expected to loan its sacred setting to any and every attempt at a union. Often the church is selected for sentiment, beauty of setting, or simply because it seats the most people and decorates well.

Churches would do well to inhibit these attitudes. If a marriage is a serious responsibility of a church and a sanctuary is a setting reserved for Christian worship, then weddings should be guided by the same considerations as worship in the congregation.

First, a pastor must assume that a couple wants a wedding in the church out of some tie or commitment to the Christian faith. Therefore, in expecting the blessing of the church, a couple ought at least to be willing to abide by the guidelines of that congregation. This approach also means that a church should take seriously that when it blesses, it accepts responsibility for pastoral and congregational care.

Second, a worship understanding of a wedding means that a couple is willing to undertake serious preparations for it. Most couples do this, but pastors are entitled to require it. Churches may wish to reconsider whether they want to permit weddings in which they do not have some input and guidance.

Third, considering a wedding to be worship will affect the nature of the service itself. For example, in some traditions many couples take Eucharist during the wedding. In the Baptist tradition, the Lord's Supper is a community event. Therefore, communion might be part of a wedding, but, on theological grounds, it would then be done with the entire congregation.

The same considerations could be applied to the issue of musical selections. Most ministers have a trunkful of horror stories about inappropriate music in weddings. The theology of the words of popular songs can be quite dreadful—and the message unintentional.

This same worship perspective has implications for the use of the wedding vows. We have been through a time of "do it yourself" vows. It has been customary for ministers to rephrase, rewrite, and adapt the traditional vows to modern times. In some cases this is appropriate.

Nevertheless, we should remember that part of the meaning of the event is its connections—to the past, to the larger community, and to God. Therefore, the creativity in a wedding should take place in the musical selections and the colors of the dresses, not in the alteration or adjustment of the vows. If they are paraphrased, it should be done with care that the meaning and requirements are not altered.

There are many dimensions of a wedding that correspond to the notion of dialogue. First, there are some things God says to all who are gathered for the service. The minister's homily is not merely a time for cute personal reminiscences, but also a time to remind the congregation of the promises and requirements of God. Both the use of scriptures and the setting of the service indicate that God is present and speaks. Some things the minister says in prayer as a representative of the community gives voice to the hopes and needs of the hour.

Second, there are some things the man and woman say to God. The promises they make are not merely to one another, but first in obedience to God. The loss of this transcendent dimension in marriage is precursor to the loss of our sense of the wedding as worship and not merely civil ceremony. A couple not only makes commitments to one another, but also responds to what God has revealed to us about a way of life.

Third, there are some things the man and woman say to one another. The dialogue is also a human conversation between two people. They have met, dated, and determined to make permanent their relationship. But now they come to formalize this through ritual worship. Theirs is not a contract but a covenant.

Finally, there are some things the community says. Some of these things are said to the couple simply by their presence in the service. They lend symbolic support, affirmation, and blessing. Some things the community says to themselves, however. The worship service of a wedding is an occasion of covenant renewal among those present. It is a time of reflection upon the relationships in the lives of those present, and in particular their marriage commitments.

While it is laudable that many people repeat their wedding vows in worship services as an act of recommitment, the wedding itself is the symbolic and ritual occasion where that takes place. Whenever we witness the vows, we reenter their purpose. There is always "Yes" or "No" required of all who are married.

The wedding is part of the dialogue of worship that connects us to the past and draws us to new possibilities of worship and renewal in the present. Through the reaffirmation of covenant that takes place in its ritual, we are invited to look at our own relationships anew and to reflect upon them. It reminds us that life with God is lived out in the "between" of human relationships in all their complexity, complications, and possibility.

The Funeral as Worship

Funerals are the purest example of the unpredictable and uncontrollable that happen in ministry. They come, sometimes suddenly, and are almost always inconvenient. There is often little time for adequate preparation.

Yet, a fitting word must be spoken. A family must negotiate the most trying of circumstances—a permanent loss. Sometimes death brings a crisis for the entire community of faith. A child dies unexpectedly, or a beloved leader expires. A teenager dies in an accident, and now an entire community comes face to face with Job's unanswered question, "Why is light given to one who cannot see the way, whom God has fenced in?" (Job 3:23).

Pastoral occasions are crisis occasions. The occasion provides a challenge to the leaders of worship. What word is fitting at such a time? What preposition can adequately describe an event at which one most commonly hears ministers say, "There are no words for a time like this," and then proceed to talk for ten minutes?

There is a preposition for the funeral—it is the word "beyond." Here is an occasion where Christian worship takes the participants and helps them in the here and now. It also leads them to the very edge of human language and understanding and peers across the gulf of death. We look beyond the present in faith to the future.

The concept of funeral as worship helps us here. Ritual structures the "chaos moving on the face of the deep." The *structure* of worship is of great help in negotiating the terrible "letting go" that is a funeral.

A funeral is unique. It is affected and shaped in part by the "word made flesh" in the life of the person who died. Yet, we do not abandon the faith for the crisis. It is too tempting to abandon the essentially worshipful character of our gathering for reasons of sentimentalism.

A good funeral is both personal and an act of worship toward God. It is not always necessary to abandon the church year. At Christmas or Holy Week, a skillful worship leader is able to find themes and emphases that weave together the themes of those great seasons with the needs of the hour.

In a funeral the congregation is called upon not only to surround a family with its tears, but also to confess its faith. Liturgical worship is at its greatest in the funeral, for the liturgy has the power to carry persons through a time when spontaneity is at low ebb.

Worship speaks "beyond" our present experience because it is ordered at a time when all is disorder. It gives us a voice, in familiar, reassuring words, when we are unable to hold up our end of the conversation. There is nothing to say, but we are able to say what has been said through the ages in scripture and confession.

Like all worship, the primary emphasis is responding to God. What has God said for this hour? There are two opposite dangers to a funeral. First, there might not be an appropriate word. We might ask or answer the wrong questions. When this occurs, there is a sense of "disconnection." The service has an air of triviality. We state the obvious, but there is an aura of banality and emptiness. Even when the words express the great truths of the faith that we know to be true and meaningful, somehow, coming out of the speaker's mouth at that moment, they sound hollow. It was not the right word *for that moment.*

Second, we might err in the other direction, and in our zeal to worship God and not say too much that is inappropriate, we might fail to make it a personal word. The service might ignore the person's life or speak generically about the individual. It is also possible to turn the individual into a saint who is unrecognizable to those who knew the person best. In proper worship these elements are brought into balance. The service itself can reflect who they were.

It is also possible that the funeral is not a transcendent occasion. A sentimental, overly person-centered service may help us to feel better, but only connection with the resources of the faith can sustain us for the long haul, and there is a vast difference between the two.

Philosopher Nicholas Wolterstorff experienced the death of a son and kept a journal of his experience of grief. Of the worship at the funeral he wrote:

> Elements of the gospel which I had always thought would console did not. They did something else, something important, but not that. It did not console me to be reminded of the hope of resurrection. If I had forgotten that hope, then it would indeed have brought light into my life to be reminded of it. But I did not think of death as a bottomless pit. I did not grieve as one who has no hope. Yet Eric is gone, here and now he is gone; now I cannot talk with him, now I cannot see him, now I cannot hug him, now I cannot hear of his plans for the future. That is my sorrow.[8]

Like all good worship, there is balance in a service so that not only the familiar and the reassuring, but also the difficult, the mystery, and the unresolved are touched. This gives voice to that which we cannot articulate. Smooth, glib reassurance has the sound not of comfort but of unreality.

Wolterstorff said, "I dreaded the prospect, but the funeral gave rest to my soul. It did not console me for Eric's absence.

Instead it sank deep into me the realization that my son's death is not all there is."[9] He told of speaking briefly about his son, thanking those gathered for coming, and expressing his deep feelings of love and anguish for his son. Then he described the end of the service, where we hear the depths of worship—that its meaning is not confined to us, our power, or our efforts. "Afterwards, I found I had the voice to sing the final hymn."[10]

The transcendent quality of worship is our surrender of control and our willingness to enter the mystery of presence with God at a time even when God seems absent. We sing and cry, laugh and lament. Good worship helps us to do them all.

Funerals are occasions that overwhelm our ability to console with words. But they are also transcendent occasions. A pastor gains a hearing that is rarely experienced in ordinary worship services. The presence of death brings the aura of eternity into the room.

There is always need for ritual on occasions of grief. Such ritual may be formal or informal. On many occasions, people will not have had occasion to do so—they live far away, they were in the hospital when the funeral took place, or they were estranged from the family.

Ritual worship is a way to "help them through." Such ritual need not be in a corporate or formal setting, of course. Pastoral ritual can be improvised on occasion. A time of prayer by the graveside can be a meaningful way to assist someone who was not able to attend the service. A brief memorial time at the bedside can assist a grief-stricken person to cope with sudden loss when the funeral is too far away.

Grief work is facilitated by ritual occasions that provide opportunity to remember the dead and name them again. Our church recently had a memorial worship service at Christmas on a Sunday afternoon. Participants brought a favorite picture of a loved one. Scripture, litany, and prayer framed the service, but there was also time for the telling of stories. It was a simple, powerful, and touching time.

The power of a funeral is fully in its connection to and dialogue with the great Christian tradition that proclaims faith, hope, and love that will abide forever. In daily life they are good intentions. At the graveside they constitute the existential power of life through the presence of the Holy Spirit that enables us to affirm that this is not a grim and hopeless moment, but one of transition and connection to eternity.

Other Transitions

Worship is a vehicle of response to God that gives voice to us in the crises of life. This truth also applies to occasions other than weddings and funerals. We need ritual occasions to mark the crisis moments of life. Crises need not be merely catastrophic events; they also refer to the ordinary, expected transitions in life—birth, adolescence, graduation, and retirement.

The preposition that comes to mind in life's transitions is "through." Worship enables us to find our way through the transitions of life.

An example of this type of worship is the dedication service. In many traditions infant baptism is practiced as a sign of grace and of the covenant love of God that precedes our response. Evangelical groups such as Baptists who practice believer's baptism have a corresponding practice called the "dedication."

The dedication is a way to mark a beginning. It is to acknowledge that God is at work prior to conversion. A dedication service is not primarily "dedication of" the child so much as it is the commitment of the parents to follow Christian principles in raising the child and a commitment of the church to sustain and nurture the family in their effort.

Transitions are occasions in which worship speaks. Through ritual, symbol, and response, the dialogue between persons and God is nurtured and enabled despite the great disruptions transitions represent. Throughout the seasons of life, the nature of that communication may change, but at every point our lives require connection with the living God. Whether our worship is the week-in, week-out routine of Sunday praise or the crisis-centered speech of the funeral, it gives us voice.

Learning to pray and to worship are life for the Christian. With the Psalmist we can say:

> Where can I go from your spirit? Or where can I flee from your presence? If I ascend to heaven, you are there; if I make my bed in Sheol, you are there. If I take the wings of the morning and settle at the farthest limits of the sea, even there your hand shall lead me, and your right hand shall hold me fast. If I say, "Surely the darkness shall cover me, and the light around me become night," even the darkness is not dark to you; the night is as bright as the day, for darkness is as light to you. (Ps 139:7-12)

The conversation between God and God's people reaches into every corner of life, speaks in every occasion, and weaves together the most solitary moments with the singing of all the saints of eternity.

The prepositions of worship are almost invisible to us, for they function to connect us with something higher. In good worship, we are not conscious of the funeral liturgy or the wedding service order. We are freed to make connection to the larger truths God grants us. Worship enables us in various ways—within, together, with, between, beyond, or through—to connect our lives with the larger reality revealed to us in Jesus the Christ.

Notes

[1] Genesis 12:7-8, 26:25, 35:7.

[2] Don Saliers, "Worship and Celebration," in *Dictionary of Pastoral Care and Counseling*, ed. Rodney J. Hunter (Nashville: Abingdon Press, 1990) 1339-42.

[3] Ibid.

[4] Paul Tillich, *Dynamics of Faith* (New York: Harper & Row Publishers, 1957) 41-54.

[5] Dietrich Bonhoeffer, *Life Together: A Discussion of Christian Fellowship* (San Francisco: Harper & Row Publishers, 1954) 76.

[6] Ibid., 77.

[7] Thomas I. Day, *Dietrich Bonhoeffer on Christian Community and Common Sense* (Toronto: The Edwin Mellen Press, 1982) 99-100.

[8]Nicholas Wolsterstorff, *Lament for a Son* (Grand Rapids: Wm. B. Eerdman's Publishing Co., 1987) 31.

[9]Ibid., 38.

[10]Ibid., 40.

Conclusion

Principles
for Dialogic Worship

Gary Furr and Milburn Price

The intent of this book has been to present an understanding of worship—at its heart and at its best—as being dialogic in nature. The tapestry of worship is formed by the various threads of conversation that occur in interweaving fashion: God's Word being communicated to the gathered community (both individually and corporately), worshipers responding to God under the prompting of God's Spirit, and those same worshipers sharing with each other their understandings of their faith commitments and of the ways in which God is at work in their lives.

As a way of summarizing the ideas we have presented, we suggest the following principles for dialogic worship.

(1) *God is the focus of the conversations of dialogic worship.* Regarding the church's song, Augustine once wrote, "If there be praise, and it is not of God, it is not a hymn."[1] Augustine's declaration could be aptly paraphrased, to apply to the whole of worship: "If there be praise (or confession, petition, or response) and it is not of (or to) God, then it is not worship." It is God's Word that comes to the gathered community in worship. It is God to whom the worshipers respond, and it is God about whom they talk to each other.

(2) *In dialogic worship, the worshipers are active (and interactive) participants.* Passive listening and observing, in a "spectator" mindset, are antithetical to an understanding of worship as dialogue. Each member of the congregation should actively engage in the conversation, listening intently for ways in which the Word of God might be encountered in a personal way and responding to God appropriately throughout the ebb and flow of the conversation.

(3) *In dialogic worship, the Word of God may be encountered through a variety of "messengers."* It has been customary in evangelical worship to identify scripture and sermon as the sources for "hearing God's Word" in the context of worship. Though these are, indeed, important and primary sources, they are not the only ones. Music, drama, symbols, and silence all provide opportunities for God to communicate with waiting hearts and minds.

(4) *Dialogic worship includes and touches the relationships of human participants with one another as well as their relationship to God.* Human ends and human benefits in worship are always secondary to the primary end of response to God, but wise leaders are aware that their efforts may contribute to or detract from the spiritual formation of members. In worship, participants encounter and respond to God. Additionally, fully dialogic worship also gives voice to their concerns, expresses their needs, provides opportunity for them to affirm their faith together, challenges them to grow individually and collectively, and builds community.

(5) *Dialogic worship implies a conversation between the content and tradition of the historic faith and the contemporary gathering of worshipers.* Worship is a teaching conversation—a dialogue between the great stream of witnesses and those struggling to incorporate what is perennial about that stream in the present. Dialogic worship, therefore, does not merely serve pragmatic ends; it instructs, shapes, and invites participants into a reality that provides an alternative to the dominant culture. While connection with the idioms and media of the current culture are important, worship is also about the formation of an identity, as the body of Christ, that is in tension with that culture.

(6) *The primary functions of music in worship are to facilitate the dialogue and to contribute to that dialogue.* Though aesthetic delight, personal enjoyment, and opportunity for a performer to share a talent may be by-products of the use of music in worship, none of these should be a primary purpose. Unless music can make a meaningful contribution to the dialogue in worship, it should be omitted. It would be better for music to be absent than for it to be an interruption or distraction.

(7) *Structures for worship services should embody a dialogic principle.* While allowing for a variety of models, this principle emphasizes the importance of consciously incorporating into every worship service opportunities for the various conversations that have been discussed in this book to take place. As a building is weakened by the removal of any major structural element, absence of any one of the three primary "directions" of conversation (God to worshipers, worshipers to God, and worshipers to each other) weakens the structure—and enactment—of worship.

(8) *Worship is a conversation that is relevant to and connects with all dimensions of life.* Worship is not a compartment of life confined to Sunday morning. It connects with all dimensions of human experience. Through the use of meaningful ritual, worship is a means by which human crises, developmental issues, and transitions are brought into connection with the resources of the gospel. For that reason, worship can take many forms, from very personal and individual to highly specialized corporate occasions. All of these forms, whether private devotion or a wedding, share the same essential character of worship.

● ● ●

The authors hope that worship leaders sense both the importance and the privilege of leading worship and that worshipers recognize the extraordinary opportunity they have to assemble as a community in the presence of God. Matters of great consequence are at stake whenever a community of faith gathers to meet God. While worship has its detractors, who accuse it of everything from irrelevance to lifelessness, Christian worship is alive and well.

Christian worship is alive because, in its essence, it is a conversation between two living realities—the one true, eternal God and the body of Christ, the church. Because worship is a conversation and not a mere review of the past, it is dynamic, unpredictable, and open-ended.[2] Who knows what might transpire on any given day when a group of believers hears and responds to the Word of God!

This dialogical aspect of worship should cause leaders to come to the task of worship planning with both excitement and hope. The Christian story is one whose final chapter has been anticipated but not yet written. It is still being lived by the community. In the drama of the Christian life, worship may be thought of as the script through which the Author of us all calls forth and responds to the deepest and most important longings in us. The lines in the script invite not so much that we memorize them as that we internalize them. When we take them into ourselves, the words of worship express that which we most deeply long to know and experience—the Living God.

Notes

[1]Augustine, "In psalmum lxxii, I," in James McKinnon, *Music in Early Christian Literature* (Cambridge: Cambridge University Press, 1989) 158.

[2]This approach is not merely a device for theological understanding. Dialogue is at the heart of scripture itself. Walter Brueggemann notes that "the Old Testament in its theological articulation is characteristically dialectical and dialogical, and not transcendentalist." Therefore, he contends, Israel's faith is an ongoing conversation with God and with each other. In Israel's God-talk we find an essential restlessness and openness. See Walter Brueggemann, *Theology of the Old Testament* (Minneapolis: Fortress Press, 1997) 83-84.